A Coach's Guide to Team Building

Coaching Psychology for Professional Practice

Series editor: Dr Manfusa Shams, FHEA, AFBPsS, C.Psychol, CSci

A Coach's Guide to Team Building

Understanding Functions, Structure and Leadership

Helen Smith and Tony Wall

Mc
Graw
Hill

Open University Press

Open University Press
McGraw Hill
Unit 4
Foundation Park
Roxborough Way
Maidenhead
SL6 3UD

email: emea_uk_ireland@mheducation.com
world wide web: www.mheducation.co.uk

Executive Editor: Beth Summers
Editorial Assistant: Hannah Jones
Content Product Manager: Ali Davis

A catalogue record of this book is available from the British Library

ISBN-13: 9780335250677
ISBN-10: 033525067X
eISBN: 9780335250684

Library of Congress Cataloging-in-Publication Data
CIP data applied for

Typeset by Transforma Pvt. Ltd., Chennai, India

Fictitious names of companies, products, people, characters and/or data that may be used herein (in case studies or in examples) are not intended to represent any real individual, company, product or event.

Praise page

"The issue of working with teams in a coaching way is very much on the agenda and this book captures the key points of what this means in practice. The book takes the reader through the challenges of working with teams, the various contexts and understanding of what team effectiveness means. It considers behaviour, both positive and negative, within teams and for the coaching manager and the book draws on good evidence to back the arguments up. This book provides support for team leaders, managers, supervisors and practitioners alike and therefore it is a 'must read' for all those in these roles."

Professor Bob Garvey, Leeds Business School, UK

"This book confirms to me that great team leaders and team managers have a coaching mindset, coaching skills and coaching behaviours at their core. This book demonstrates how best to be 'coach-minded' and gives lots of advice on how to be an excellent manager as coach (MAC) in terms of fostering confidence, humility, learning and exchange within a team.
I like the way the key aspects, in each chapter, are clearly defined through easy to follow figures and short summaries of key theorists work, followed by a psychological underpinning section, with a supporting case study and reflective questions. I felt clearly coached through each stage of each chapter."

Dr Jenni Jones, Associate Professor in Coaching and Mentoring, University of Wolverhampton, UK

Contents

Figures and tables

Figures

Tables

Series editor's foreword

The Coaching Psychology for Professional Practice series aims to promote professional practice in coaching psychology. Each book in this series is expected to address a critical area in coaching practice, underpinned by relevant theories, with a focus on 'application and practice'.

This book, *A Coach's Guide to Team Building: Understanding Functions, Structure and Leadership*, by Helen Smith and Tony Wall exemplifies the powerful influence of coaching in leadership behaviour. Despite the popular notion of a leader as a coach, this idea has never been fully researched or discussed. The critical issue of 'coaching' itself as an appropriate leadership and management style is argued to support leadership development. Each chapter showcases a different case study, and the discussion is underpinned by relevant psychological theory, followed by reflective questions.

I hope this book will bring a fresh perspective on leadership coaching and team building, and provide a practical guide for practitioners. I welcome Helen Smith and Tony Wall's dedicated scholarly work and tireless efforts to articulate critical and complex issues, simplicity in delivering practice-related reflective narrative, and their bold approach to embracing coaching as a leadership and management style.

Dr Manfusa Shams, SFHEA, CPsychol, AFBPsS, CSci
Series editor, Coaching Psychology for Professional Practice, McGraw-Hill
and Open International Publishing limited (OU Press).

Preface

Effective teams demand sharing, good communication, openness of approach and personal engagement to create the necessary cohesion and collaboration. The modern team environment demands a highly competent team leader and manager who is capable of dealing with its inherent diversity, leveraging widening demographics and the merging of organizational hierarchies due to the compression of role responsibilities and scarcity of resources. This dynamic team environment and the interplay between multiple elements have contributed to the evolution of the traditional bureaucratic style of management into a higher proficiency of inclusive and more engaging leadership with an active coaching style at its core. In this context, there is an assumption that team managers and leaders will utilize coaching to successfully tackle the complexity of modern teams using conventional coaching interventions. While each team brings together a unique blend of individuals, this may create an unrealistic expectation when set against a backdrop of constant change, since the assumption that managers and team leaders can coach and will coach carries a huge question mark.

This book aims to support team leaders, managers, supervisors and practitioners by summarizing the potential contributions required from a coaching perspective to facilitate a fully functioning team. On completion of each section a psychological explanation is offered, with reflective activities for the reader to ponder in relation to *their own* team. Please note, the authors are not psychology-trained experts and therefore these explanations are based on curiosity and seeking a rationale to achieve success using a coaching approach. The book begins with an investigation into the likely team challenges that may identify why a team does not function optimally. This insight then builds on some of the traditionally explored and accepted models of team effectiveness such as the Team Leadership Framework (Fleishman 1992), the Team Basics Model (Katzenbach and Smith 1999) and Real Team Effectiveness (Hackman 2002). This also provides a solid platform of understanding for how to lead teams effectively, as exemplified by the work of Edmondson (2012), which focused on the impact of team emotional intelligence and the ability of the team to become an effective and cohesive entity. The research output shared in this book will add a further layer to the aforementioned foundational team models, sharing insights from 30 forward-thinking (modern-day) managers and team leaders who lead and manage their teams from a coaching (style) perspective.

The book progresses to the exploration of the various elements that can externally impact a team and its ability to function fully. How leaders and managers can engineer a conducive team environment to the advantage of each team member will be reviewed.

The authors advocate why coaching is regarded as an appropriate style of leadership and management in addressing current, modern-day potential challenges that a team may face. These insights will be underpinned using insights from a psychological perspective with an explanatory rationale. Coaching is still in its infancy in establishing its credibility in a wider area of application in teams, and it is hoped this book will add to that endeavour in a small way.

We hope you engage with the self-reflections that appear throughout the chapters, and find the self-assessment and the models presented towards the end of the book helpful in developing your fully functional (*dream*) team and creating a positive environment for the future success of team members and your organization.

Helen and Tony

References

Edmondson, A.C. (2012). Learning to team, *Leadership Excellence*, 29(8): 6.

Fleishman, E.A. (1992). Taxonomic efforts in the description of leader behavior: a synthesis and functional interpretation, *Leadership Quarterly*, 2(4): 245–87.

Hackman, J.R. (2002). *Leading Teams: Setting the Stage for Great Performance*. Boston, MA: Harvard Business School Press.

Katzenbach, J.R. and Smith, D.K. (1999). *The Wisdom of Teams: Creating the High-Performance Organization*. London: Harper Business.

Chapter	Summary	Keywords/Concepts
Chapter 1 Exploring team challenge	This chapter explores the origins of team challenge, establishing the importance of its recognition for team members and the team leader.	Diversity Dynamics Building trust Alignment Time Ownership Responsibility
Chapter 2 Team context	This chapter highlights the environmental demands which make team challenge a pressing issue to understand, appreciate and manage.	Resource scarcity Employee demands Team configuration
Chapter 3 Understanding team effectiveness	This chapter reviews current models for team effectiveness and the academic literature to provide the reader with a solid platform for understanding what is defined as team effectiveness, and the nature of team effectiveness in a modern team.	Team effectiveness Enabling structures Safe team environment Clarity of direction Interpersonal focus Collaboration and trust Perceived outcomes
Chapter 4 Individual behaviour and its impact on the team	This chapter gives an appreciation of the behavioural impact of the team leader and team members, offering a rationale as to why sometimes things do not go smoothly.	Managing and leading Team cohesion, engagement, collaboration and sharing Team member perception Organizational support, behaviour and management practice of the team leader
Chapter 5 Understanding dysfunctional behaviour	This chapter explores team challenge attributed to dysfunctional behaviour experienced by managers as coaches, plus the potential origins of dysfunctional behaviour and its impact within the team.	Understanding dysfunctional behaviour Organizational culture creating dysfunction Manager influence
Chapter 6 Demands on manager and team leader	Managers and team leaders carry the burden of delivering the organizational strategy through the individuals in their charge. Multiple authorities (CIPD, CMI, ILM) inform us they are also best placed to deal with this task.	Environmental demands Manager expectations Employee expectations

Chapter	Summary	Keywords/Concepts
Chapter 7 **The coaching** **approach**	This chapter outlines the research findings related to the experience of a MAC in dealing with team challenge, reinforced and validated by published literature with a coaching psychology explanation.	Manager as coach Response Understanding Alignment Relationship Mindset Process and systems Trust
Chapter 8 **Insights and** **recommendations**	This chapter reviews the insights and recommendations drawn from the interviews, and shares multiple examples and quotations to illustrate the additions that can be concluded to supplement the effectiveness models we are familiar with.	Dealing with team challenge Trust, accountability and commitment Creating a safe environment, Clarity of direction Coaching interpersonal focus Problem-solving and enhanced learning Collaborative team working Perceived outcomes and improved learning capabilities
Chapter 9 **MAC:** **development of** **templates**	This chapter consolidates the findings and effectiveness insights leading to the development of templates, models and self-assessments. It also gives explanation of the potential application of these tools and how you may wish to adapt and tailor them to your team, organization and purpose. These insights are shared with the valuable underpinning with coaching psychology research and knowledge.	Importance of knowing your team Being coach-minded Conduct of the manager as coach Leadership Characteristics of manager as coach Templates Models Checklist Self-assessment Practitioner application

1 Exploring team challenge

Summary

This chapter explores the origins of team challenge, establishing the importance of its recognition for all team members, especially that of the team leader. The chapter takes the lived experiences of managers and leaders dealing with challenge in a variety of contexts – e.g. higher education institutions, the public sector, the military, banking and the voluntary sector to name a few – that they reported on in their daily management and leadership of a team. The topics covered here as creating challenge are those most commonly identified by managers and leaders. This list is not exhaustive, but hopefully it is representative of a typical team environment in modern society.

Keywords: diversity, dynamics, building trust, alignment, time, ownership, responsibility

Introduction

Team working has changed radically in recent times. Teams are individually context-situated and context-sensitive environments, making each team unique. Even teams within the same organization can be different, which is a factor that a team manager or leader must be sensitive to. Modern organizations have become increasingly complex and nonlinear, and need to be strategically responsive entities, usually structured around skilled networks of highly empowered teams of knowledge workers (Kunnanatt 2016) as modern society is primarily cognitively driven (Hinsz 2015). Aligned with this complexity and a move towards flatter, more flexible structures, the team is increasingly experiencing and subjected to the dynamics of the contemporary nature of the workplace. This becomes an ever-increasingly complex environment requiring managers to respond to these changes by acquiring a new skill set to interact correctly with employees and the environment simultaneously, in support of the rapid changes, some driven in part by technological growth factors.

Work is increasingly structured around teams that solve complex problems within organizations, with teams emerging as an attractive form of organizing work through the capability of integrating varying sources of expertise to cope with increased complexity and change while drawing on the differing skill sets of team members. Teams allow the possibility of sequencing and synchronizing team tasks (Maruping et al. 2015), utilizing the interdependent expertise provided by individual team members. Teams in isolation are used as a technology to achieve tasks, goals or social objectives that cannot be accomplished individually (Hinsz 2015). Teams have been recognized as becoming increasingly dynamic in nature even before the Covid-19 pandemic, thus intensifying the managerial challenge of supporting effective team functioning. Writers such as Bushe and Chu (2011) have described this team dynamic as being fluid, due to being in a constant state of flux. With the increased reliance of organizations on teams, individual team members are required to collaborate (Edmondson 2012) inside and outside of the team and the organization itself. Teams are being recognized as the sustainable backbone of many organizations and the powerhouse that drives the activity outputs of the organization, highlighting the importance of fully functioning teams and the expectations being put upon them. In addition, teams are now increasingly complex (Fairhurst and Connaughton 2014) and irrational, mirroring the demands being made of them, which when supplemented by the complexity of the individual team members creates the new norm of continuous change and potential challenge for all stakeholders.

Organizations are constantly striving to be more productive and successful in a competitive market (Fairhurst and Connaughton 2014), with employee work engagement being acknowledged as the key to achieving this (Engelbrecht et al. 2014). This constant striving serves to add to the increased expectations being placed on managers and leaders in how they engage team members to create an empowered team to become the organizational powerhouse. Managers and leaders must be careful not to disempower their staff (Lin 2015) by failing to engage each individual, and must be cognizant of the methods that bind individuals closer as a unified team without impeding individualism (Norreklit 2011). This is no easy task. There is a fine balance to be found in building a strong and supportive team, facilitating individual growth and development alongside team functioning. Binding team members together is potentially the first challenge a manager or team leader is faced with, especially when individual team members are recognized as a critical source of competitive advantage to promote business success – reinforcing the importance of engagement mentioned earlier. There is a notion that successful teams result in successful organizations (Lin 2015), heightening the leader/manager responsibility and personal challenge to deliver the required outcome through their team. Team leaders and managers must appreciate the importance of managing interdependence which is critical to achieving the success both of individuals within the team and of the team task. Orchestrating individual and team success simultaneously will draw on the need to manage diversity (Grint 2010, 2012) as well as integrating appropriately the unique expertise of team members (Sudhakar 2011, cited in Erkutlu 2012). There is a further need to align different cultural and behavioural characteristics (Agrawal 2012) to achieve the required *bonding or togetherness* of the team members, which is reliant on the need for mutual appreciation between team members as a bridge to this *bonding* occurring.

Aims

The task of binding team members together, setting direction and vision for the joint team activities and ensuring continuous proactivity (Maruping et al. 2015) is an indicator of engagement. Team leaders and managers are also expected to be responsible for the personal development of individual team members. This may seem an impossible task to achieve in an ever-changing environment – even more reason for team leaders and managers to understand what creates team challenge and how to recognize it immediately, put steps in place to avoid it and build a strong functioning team. This chapter aims to explore the most reported items that have the potential to create team challenge.

Diversity – as a challenge

With demographic change and increased globalization being the norm, diversity is not only inevitable but desirable to broaden the available resource pool of skilled employees (Cheng et al. 2012). The variety of skills and personalities within a team can therefore be many and varied but still need to be complementary to foster the differing ideas and ways of approaching tasks (Chughtai and Buckley 2011); some believe this difference enables innovation and creativity. As a result, work teams are increasingly diversified and cosmopolitan, requiring leaders to lead and managers to manage teams with increased cultural diversity, ethnicity, nationality, differing values, mindsets and strengths. These can play out in negative or positive ways within a team, thereby posing issues for the team leader/manager to navigate. Because of this diversity, managers and leaders need to administer interdependence between team members to achieve individual success within the team and facilitate support for the completion of (seamless) team tasks. A diverse team may be hampered in achieving its goals (Boerner et al. 2011; Agrawal 2012; Sommers 2012: 60 – 'the greater the diversity in group the broader the range of aspirations and values to accommodate'; Hentschel et al. 2013) if diversity is allowed to damage team functioning by creating negative potential and a greater propensity for conflict (Cheng et al. 2012).

This area of potential team conflict and its link to team functionality is of specific interest in this book and will be revisited later, drawing on research into how managers and team leaders address these possible conflict flash points through the application of coaching vs. non-coaching styles. The impact of diversity on team functioning reveals that team members with a more open attitude and an accepting mindset view diversity as an advantage and try to learn and encompass different ways of approaching tasks (Agrawal 2012). Conversely, team members not willing to learn from one another, or not willing to be open to the acceptance of differences and change, can create conflict and division which impacts on team functioning in a negative sense. In other words, the team can become dysfunctional. Relationship conflict has a detrimental effect on individuals and subsequently the team (Hentschel et al. 2013),

Table 1.1 Team challenge as reported by managers and leaders

Challenge	Interviewee responses
conflict	51
attitudes (bad/negative)	38
change	23
time	9
ownership	8
trust	4
miscellaneous	15

whereas some believe conflict is healthy for idea generation within a team (Santos and Passos 2013).

Thirty semi-structured interviews with modern-day managers and leaders (see Appendix item 1, illustrating their individual profiles) explored the present-day team environment with an insight into the greatest challenges faced within teams, as shown in Table 1.1.

Over half the challenges reported by the managers and leaders relating to the individual behaviour of members within the team refer to conflict (51 reports) and attitude (38 reports). Change was often reported to be imposed on team members and the manager/team leader without consultation, excluding them from the decision-making process. This could result from the fast-paced (change) environment discussed earlier, but relates certainly to enforced change, whatever the driver. Some managers reported challenge as having a negative influence, while others considered challenge as motivating, inspiring and positive. Again, mindset has an impact on this from a manager perspective. Considering these insights, managers and team leaders would do well to recognize and appreciate the influence each team member can have (Wood et al. 2011) and address potential challenges individually for the benefit of the team. This enabling of team members to perform fully provides the confidence to influence positively other team members to take responsibility for managing team diversity (Paustain-Underdahl et al. 2013) and accept diversity on a day-by-day basis. However, it is the manager or team leader's responsibility to establish the positive platform for acceptance of diversity and appreciation of its benefits for the team members. How this may be done will be referred to later in the book.

Dynamics – as a challenge

Team dynamics can be affected by multiple factors from inside and outside of the team. The internal well-being and social support within a team is linked to team-working ability (Amos and Klimoski 2014). Teams have emerged as an essential means of organizing work tasks as they are better able to manage large amounts of information and are better resourced compared to individuals. Teams also facilitate the management of interdependence and sequencing of complex activities (Belbin 1969). Teams evolve for different reasons, bringing together the requisite (unique) skills and personalities to achieve the desired team outputs, while acknowledging that team members who work independently cannot contribute to the achievement of the team output without the input from each other team member. Teams that work well together are linked to higher levels of job satisfaction and lower absenteeism compared to those not working in a fully functional team. This highlights the requirement for managers to achieve a fully functioning status to achieve the desired deliverables from an individual, team and organizational perspective.

Positive team dynamics rely on an element of trust between teammates (Nielsen and Randall 2012) which influences their engagement in joint decision-making and their problem-solving ability (Maruping et al. 2015). This trust is fundamental to team functioning by promoting cooperation, engagement and increased motivation resulting in positive performance outputs. The presence of a positive team dynamic encourages loyalty between team members and a desire to share thoughts and openness towards teammates. Such positive team dynamics can create a mutually beneficial environment and set the scene for good working relationships (Oktug 2013) between team members and the team leader, facilitating a positive environment for constructive feedback, supportive day-to-day communication and reduced opportunities for deviant or undesirable behaviour.

The role of the manager/team leader in building this positive team environment relies heavily on individual and team trustworthiness (Buvik and Tvedt 2017) to deliver the required team outputs. Managers and leaders, as behavioural exemplars as well as team architects, are ideally placed to foster this positive environmental context to develop trust through alignment of team dynamics and culture plus ultimately positive team behaviour and functionality.

Building trust – as a challenge

Trust is not usually an instant feeling one has upon meeting someone or joining a team or when working alongside other team members. When we think of those we trust, they are generally those who have been part of our circle for some time, and we may have had multiple interactions in a variety of contexts and situations. It is this repeated experience of the individual concerned that enables us to build the trust that we feel towards them. When we consider this in a team context, we can appreciate it is not an instant outcome and we as team leaders and managers need to create opportunities for trust to develop and grow in our teams.

Trust is well researched in team relationships and is known to affect knowledge sharing (Peng and Lin 2016) – that is to say we may hold things back from those we do not trust. Trust in one's supervisor, team leader or manager is also linked to work engagement (Engelbrecht et al. 2014) and is key to successful

Figure 1.1 Impact of trust within a team

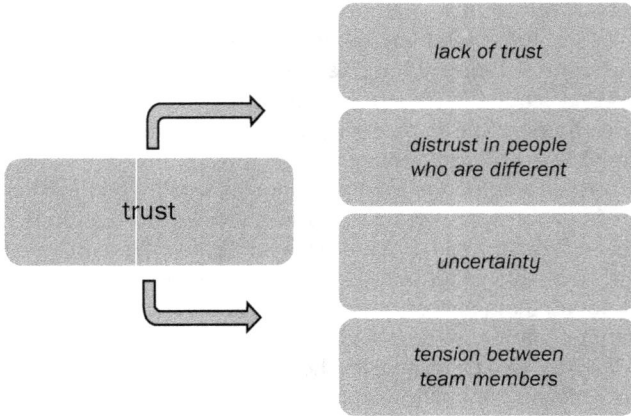

working relationships. Trust in a team context is based on the belief or otherwise that team members have good intentions as well as having confidence (or not) in the capability and character of the other team members, including the team leader. Where this trust does not exist, uncertainty prevails, sharing is inhibited and engagement between team members diminishes, which can lead to tensions between team members. Trust can impact several levels of effectiveness within a team as endorsed by the 30 managers and leaders interviewed – as illustrated in Figure 1.1.

Establishing trust and getting team members to trust one another was the reported challenge associated with *people being different* and *not trusting one another*, leading to *uncertainty* and *lack of trust* creating *tension between team members*. From these statements it is obvious that a manager or leader needs to establish a trust environment if the team is to function and deliver for everyone involved.

Alignment – as a challenge

Teams can be described as the business architecture of organizations, which is an appropriate metaphor where individual team members can be likened to the scaffolding of an organization (Hyland 2013), supporting the organization through the provision of specific skills and activities, while the team itself provides the framework and direction and coordination for these activities, through individual team members. The building blocks (Wilson 2007) that support the operation and cultural makeup of the organization to which individual employees belong (Wiedow and Konradt 2011) are the teams, the people who make up the teams and the team leader. Contemporary work arrangements place a heavy focus on the willingness of individual team members to rise to the occasion (Wiedow and Konradt 2011), to step up and be an effective and supportive team member. Expanding on the importance of the effective team construct, teams need individuals with the propensity and desire to engage and perform. Performance outputs and aspired outcomes are more likely to be achieved if individuals and teams are aligned with the aims and objectives of the organization (Amos and Klimoski 2014). Team members, though, must be willing to align with these aims and objectives (Rutti et al. 2012). The concept of alignment as essential for people to work together in working relationships was first reported by Tuckman (1965) when describing the forming of a team. As an endorsement to Tuckman, Edmondson (2012) observed also that being part of a team may require individuals to respond, to create, to work with one another, to combine their efforts and abilities, to refine processes, to deliver outcomes, to integrate and share knowledge and provide products or services for specific needs.

Being part of a team demands participation (Fairhurst and Connaughton 2014; Karaçivi and Demirel 2014; Zoltan 2015) from each team member to step up, to contribute, to understand the task in hand, to possess a willingness to work with colleagues plus an ability to align and focus on the desired team output. The phenomenon of this alignment from a psychological and group dynamics perspective reveals that the team leader needs to positively influence individual team members to be attracted towards working together whatever the output purpose of the team (Wageman et al. 2012). This achievement of total alignment engineered by the manager to enable functional interdependence appears to be critical to team functioning (CIPD 2022 and the CIPD report on the role of line managers referred to them as the 'critical conduits of learning'; Ellinger 2013) while the focus on teams as a bound together and stable set of individuals interdependent for a common purpose is often cited as critical (Kim 2014). This could also be interpreted as alignment.

From analysis of the elements that contribute to effective team functioning, this requires multiple facets to be aligned – namely attitudes, opinions and aspirations – each of which may represent an individual challenge for a manager/team leader to engineer. But if a manager or leader is committed to engineering team efficiency, misalignment and many resultant work problems will be avoided through correct team environment and task setup. This accentuates the need for the manager to align and dovetail individual skills and activities to *engineer* and set up the team to function fully (Buvik and Tvedt 2017). This alignment may not evolve naturally or immediately between team members and may demand foresight and effort from the manager to align a fully functioning team, but additionally the manager/leader requires time for this alignment based on trust to flourish. This brings us to the next challenge that managers and leaders reported, relating to the time available to facilitate and enable the bonding and mutual appreciation for this to occur.

Time – as a challenge

The pace of activity demanded of team members in the modern environment has dramatically increased, making the availability of quality time even more valuable. Conversely, a scarcity of time may impact the ability to achieve and

Figure 1.2 Time constraints within a modern team environment

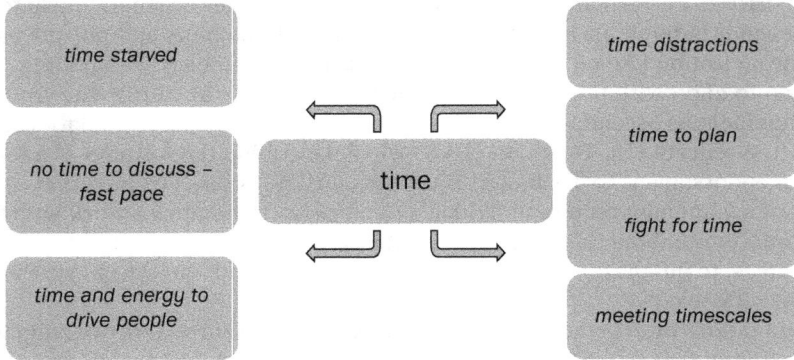

address all the potential challenges that require immediate attention. Time pressure on individual performance is a common occurrence and impacts team objectives (Maruping et al. 2015) thereby adding a further challenge to the growing list for managers and team leaders to address. Time pressure is also known to affect the engagement of individuals, sometimes creating added stress and potentially burnout: the resultant negative side of being overly engaged. The implication of this time constraint reported by managers (see Figure 1.2) has led to undue pressures through having to deliver output to deadlines with insufficient time allowance for feedback and team member support. Constructive feedback is essential to achieve individual growth and attainment of personal and team improvements. The impact of no feedback can be expensive and disastrous. Lack of time as a challenge is very real and urgent in many team contexts, especially when we consider the pace of change that feedback may need to keep up with, by potentially not allowing time for consideration before a response is required.

Time constraints are reported to create a loss of timely and appropriate feedback which could make a difference to the development of an individual and therefore the team. Furthermore, managers not having time to prepare or administer constructive conversations for feedback opportunities may act as a barrier to efficient individual and team functionality. This situation can result in the manager or team leader themselves creating a bottleneck within the team. The issue of time has been researched and mentioned by many authors, as summarized in Table 1.2, supporting the reports from the modern-day managers and leaders.

As endorsed by the interviewees, the stressors related to task, environment and social factors impinge on performance issues via threats, time pressures, task load, noise, crowding, performance pressure and ambiguity (Chughtai and Buckley 2011); these are expressed in the data as *distractions, fast pace, time to discuss*. In addition, a 2012 report established that relationship building is most successful when trust and respect *emerge over time*, which is harder to achieve when time is starved (Driskell et al. 2017). Where teams are subject

Table 1.2 Challenges reported by managers as supported by published authors

Interview data	Supporting established research
time to discuss	**Buvik and Tvedt 2017**–with no time to share and discuss, projects may suffer, be poorly coordinated and not be successful
time and energy to drive people	**CIPD 2015**–responsibility of managers to make time for team members
time to plan	**Buljac-Samardžić 2012**–removing the roadblocks that impede high performance and facilitating interpersonal relationships
pressure	**Ciporen 2015**–under multiple pressures, leaders often find themselves, in the words of Robert Kegan (1998) *in over their heads*
fast pace	**Ciporen 2015**–today's leaders operate in complex and competitive environments where they are responsible for not only *demonstrating quick results* but also leading and developing teams and showing an ability to grow talent and work effectively across cultures
fight for space	**Pulakos et al. 2015**–the supervisor becomes a developer of individuals, adopting an *on-the-job* learning approach using the *day-to-day* interaction as a developmental tool to enhance employee engagement and performance
starved	**Peters & Carr 2013**–if time starved, how can you develop *comprehensive and systemic approach to support a team to maximize their collective talent and resources to effectively accomplish the work of the team?*
measurements and timescales	**Dexter 2010**–Critical Success Factors; deliver on time **Maruping et al. (2015)**
distractions	**Buljac-Samardžić 2012**–removing the roadblocks that impede high performance, facilitating interpersonal relationships

to increased stress due to time pressure to deliver, there is greater negative effect and anxiety. Time pressure potentially amplifies each stressor for every worker, all of which could impact on the ability of the individual to absorb and assimilate details and influence their performance by not having the opportunity to take ownership or responsibility for tasks. Thus, the whole team will not function to capacity as a result. Making time to bond and offer feedback is thus identified as critical within any team, for its members and for the team to function healthily. There is no substitute for the essential team-building steps to facilitate ownership and responsibility by individuals to achieve the required activities and avoid the impact on the team if they fail to respond.

Ownership and responsibility by team members – as a challenge

Taking ownership and responsibility has relevance to empowerment and engaging staff, which benefits the team in delivering their required targets and outputs. The impact of an individual not taking ownership or responsibility can create a challenge for the team leader as well as for other team members in their endeavours to complete their own tasks and the collective team tasks. Not taking ownership and addressing one's own responsibilities can create an imbalance of workload between team members, potentially leading to resentment between them. This situation is not conducive to efficient team functioning, as illustrated in Figure 1.3.

By not taking ownership we do not display commitment to our team colleagues or the team purpose, potentially creating an unfair distribution of workload. Such non-committed individuals are also reluctant to volunteer or step forward when the team is under pressure to deliver. As a result, the manager or team leader has difficulty bringing the team together as a single seamless unit, which demands difficult conversations, possibly with individuals or the whole team. Ignoring such behaviour is too easy for any manager to do, especially when the team is under pressure to deliver to a looming deadline, time starved and balancing multiple demands. However, not addressing this behaviour is unfair to team members who are committed and who do *pull their weight*. Since leading by example is important, the team leader also needs to be seen to take ownership and responsibility for their leadership or management role, which includes being fair to all team members equally and maintaining balance within the team. By not addressing ownership and responsibility issues, the manager can lose credibility and the trust of team members. In losing such credibility the manager or team leader weakens their ability to request team members to step up when required, possibly resulting in missed deadlines and an unreliable reputation for the team.

Where team members are reluctant to take ownership and responsibility, the prospect of having a team that purports to be a technology, as mentioned

Figure 1.3 Impact of not taking ownership or responsibility

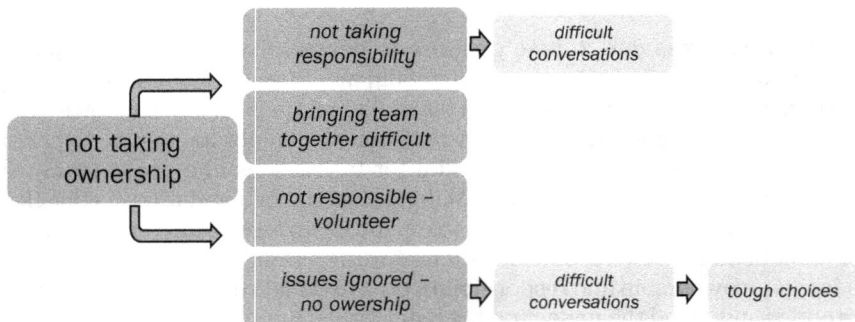

earlier (Hinsz 2015), with team members seamlessly working as a sequencing, synchronizing entity (Maruping et al. 2015), appears implausible. Authors such as Amos and Klimoski (2014) have identified that taking ownership and stepping up was a greater issue impeding the voluntary sector, where volunteer managers and leaders have little authority to manage or lead the teams of volunteers, with a strong reliance resting on their innate ability to appeal to team members to achieve desired outputs. This was endorsed by some of the managers interviewed for this book. Lack of ownership or reluctance to participate impacts total team functioning and development by inhibiting citizenship (Collins and Parker 2010). Managers and leaders reported that this creates *difficulty in bringing the team together*. It can be acknowledged and appreciated that taking the lead is considered more essential within flatter structured teams for the attainment of organizational goals (Amos and Klimoski 2014). Reluctance to take ownership and responsibility impedes the required functional behaviour of the team, with a lack of willingness creating a functional blockage which impacts the team in terms of flow and efficiency. The team no longer behaves as a synchronized technology in its own right.

Underpinning considerations

There is a psychological theory worth reviewing here called self-concordance (Sheldon and Elliot 1998), as derived from self-determination theory (Deci and Ryan 1980).

Self-concordant individuals are people who pursue life goals *with a sense* that they express their authentic choices rather than *with a sense* that they are controlled by external forces over which they have little say or influence. This could be compared to a manager or team leader knowing the various skill sets of the individual team members in their team and orchestrating these team members in such a way as to exploit their individual strengths. Thus, self-concordant goals are ones that represent the individuals' actual interests and passions as well as being aligned with central values and beliefs. In contrast, non-concordant goals are ones that are pursued with a sense of *having to*, as the person (team member) does not really enjoy or believe in that goal; they carry out the associated tasks as a chore that has to be done and is certainly not enjoyable or engaging for the person concerned. This can occur when we are ordered to carry out some task without any consultation or rationale. Self-concordance is the sense of *owning* one's personal goals. Concordance can be appreciated to affect ownership, one's willingness to volunteer, the taking of responsibility and the desire to support other team members by stepping up.

When leaders and managers understand the link between the individual's values and the goals for the team members, and align in accordance with the individual's skills, they can involve the team member through consultation, agreeing tasks together, thus facilitating authentic choice as part of the dialogue with the individual and fostering the sense of ownership we appreciate is so vital to such commitment. Managers and team leaders can use these alignment conversation opportunities to build positivity between team members, laying the platform for trust and willingness to share and support one another.

Appreciation of the importance of self-concordance will drive reason and motivation associated with individual goal setting and is an aspect the manager or team leader needs to have an overview of for each team member to ensure transparency and clarity to facilitate team task achievement.

The Self-concordance model emphasizes the extent to which an individual perceives their goal as being authentic rather than driven by external factors (that they may not share commitment to). This internal vs. external balance will determine the extent to which the individual self-integrates into the team and takes ownership for a goal. For this to occur and for team members to fully support corporate and team goals on a personal level, the team manager or team leader must present the team objectives in a congruent manner in concordance with each team member.

Top Tip: Know the value of individual team members

Case study

Jonathon was a newly appointed manager of a sales team of 23 staff of mixed abilities. The team had been without a manager for more than six months, which led the team members to believe they didn't need a replacement even though they were at the bottom of the achievement ranking nationally. They had numerous explanations for their ranking, none of which were related to their efforts. Jonathon experienced considerable resistance, and was challenged by a team member as to why they needed a manager.

Being of mixed abilities, some established and savvy team members were happy to coast along without a manager, plus new recruits were not being set a good example by the established team members. Some team members were also oblivious to the internal politics at play and the impact that the team situation could have on them and their potential achievements.

Jonathon decided to give time to assess the situation and asked each team member to arrange a personal meeting of an hour and a half to brief him on the status of the business from their perspective. He asked them to prepare a response to three questions:

- *What is the current status of the business in your area?*
- *What is the main challenge and obstacle to business growth in your area?*
- *What are the likely quick wins in your area?*

Each team member came along to their meeting with Jonathon and expressed their awareness of the business. This individual meeting also afforded an opportunity for Jonathon to assess each employee. Even though this took several days to accomplish, on completion Jonathon had a good assessment of the total business and the team members' individual commitment, needs and capabilities. The 'quick wins' response enabled Jonathon to illustrate immediately the benefit of a manager, allowing authorization of the activities required to achieve some of the quick wins. This rapidly changed the attitude of some team members and started the foundation of building trust.

Jonathon also divided the team members into 'buddy' groups to exploit the business acumen of the more established team members (which inspired them too, and illustrated trust) to support the new recruits. This forged mutual respect and appreciation between the team members and took some pressure from Jonathon himself while he dealt with more pressing issues in the team.

Jonathon then arranged a 'vision setting meeting'. This meeting was in two parts: the morning session was delivered by a motivational speaker whom Jonathon had pre-briefed about the team and what he would like them to achieve. On completion of a short motivational presentation each team member was invited to break through a wooden block (Karate style). Team members were slow to volunteer for this activity initially, but once one or two did and were successful, everyone wanted to break the wooden blocks. Team support for this activity grew as team members stepped forward, and a feeling of genuine teaming was evident. This metaphor for overcoming obstacles was discussed, with each team member expressing their feelings on smashing their wooden block, plus 'did they think they were going to break the wooden block at the start of the morning, and what had changed'. Photographs were taken as mementos and to remind the team members of the scope and magnitude of the obstacle they had faced plus what their potential could be if they tried. There followed an energized working lunch together offering an opportunity for team building.

The second part of the day related to planning and how the team planned to work together. The buddy teams were formalized openly (transparent communication) and Jonathon presented the sales status of the team, highlighting gaps and shortfalls (without blame). As they had not had a manager to guide them, the challenge was presented with honesty and openness. Support and the opinion of the team was sought on the scope of the team challenge and what could be done. The team were fully involved in the planning and decision-making, and trusted to know all the details they collectively faced. The buddy teams also presented an opportunity for a little healthy competition, something Jonathon took advantage of during his weekly and monthly communication with the team. Thereafter, each team member created their individual sales plan, aligned with their buddy team and the overall team targets, to assist in addressing the shortfalls presented by Jonathon.

While it is a known phenomenon that team members will generally overestimate what they can deliver, the process did engage each team member while fostering ownership and responsibility for the targets they had set themselves. Jonathon then talked about front loading, in the context of achievement vs. target pacing. Within one year this team moved from being ranked 49th of 50 teams in the UK to the number one national team with some amazing individual achievement contributing to their staggering team achievement.

Reflective questions

- What are the different aspects of diversity in my teams? What sorts of tensions do I observe which might be linked with those aspects of diversity? To what extent do I observe these tensions leading to team challenge?
- What aspects of diversity are not present in my teams? What might be an impact of this in relation to the way my teams work together or the way they think about or resolve problems?
- Who do I observe creates challenge in my team? What resources are they bringing?
- Who do I observe attempts to resolve challenges in my team? What resources are they bringing?
- What are the sources of trust in my teams?
- What would I say are my top three challenges presently? Who are they important to? What does that say about the source of challenge and how I might resolve it?
- Once a challenge arises in my teams, who attempts to own it until it is resolved? What might be done to strengthen a culture of this?
- Following Jonathon's case study, can I identify any examples or tips I could adopt to assist my team?
- What psychological elements did Jonathon embed in his approach to team building?

References

Agrawal, V. (2012). Managing the diversified team: challenges and strategies for improving performance, *Team Performance Management: An International Journal*, 18(7/8): 384–400. http://dx.doi.org/10.1108/13527591211281129.

Amos, B. and Klimoski, R.J. (2014). Courage: making teamwork work well, *Group & Organization Management*, 39(1): 110–28. DOI: 10.1177/1059601113520407.

Belbin, R. Meredith (1969). *The Discovery Method: An International Experiment in Retraining*. Paris: Organisation for Economic Co-operation and Development.

Boerner, S., Linkohr, M. and Kiefer, S. (2011). Top management team diversity: positive in the short run, but negative in the long run?, *Team Performance Management*, 17(7/8): 328–53.

Buljac-Samardžić, M. (2012). *Health Teams: Analyzing and Improving Team Performance in Long-Term Care*. Rotterdam: Erasmus University Rotterdam.

Bushe, G.R. and Chu, A. (2011). Fluid teams, solutions to the problems of unstable teams, *Organizational Dynamics*, 40(3): 181–8.

Buvik, M.P. and Tvedt, S.D. (2017). The influence of project commitment and team commitment on the relationship between trust and knowledge sharing in project teams, *Project Management Journal*, 48(2): 5.

Cheng, C., Chua, R.Y.J., Morris, M.W. and Lee, L. (2012). Finding the right mix: how the composition of self-managing multicultural teams' cultural value orientation influences performance over time, *Journal of Organizational Behavior*, 33(3): 389–411.

Chughtai, A.A. and Buckley, F. (2011). Work engagement, antecedents, the mediating role of learning goal orientation and job performance, *Career Development International*, 16(7): 684–705.

CIPD (Chartered Institute of Personnel and Development) (2022). *Line managers' role in supporting the people profession* [factsheet]. Available at: http://www.cipd.co.uk/hr-resources/factsheets/role-line-managers-hr.aspx (accessed 13 January 2023).

Ciporen, R. (2015). The emerging field of executive and organizational coaching: an overview, *New Directions for Adult and Continuing Education*, 2015(148): 5–15.

Collins, C.G. and Parker, S.K. (2010). Team capability beliefs over time: distinguishing between team potency, team outcome efficacy, and team process efficacy, *Journal of Occupational and Organizational Psychology*, 83(4): 1003–1023.

Dexter, B. (2010). Critical success factors for developmental team projects, *Team Performance Management: An International Journal*, 16(7/8): 343–58. http://dx.doi.org/10.1108/13527591011090637.

Driskell, T., Salas, E. and Driskell, J.E. (2017). Teams in extreme environments: alterations in team development and teamwork, *Human Resource Management Review*, 28(4): 434–49. http://dx.doi.org/10.1016/j.hrmr.2017.01.002.

Edmondson, A.C. (2012). Learning to team, *Leadership Excellence*, 29(8): 6.

Ellinger, A.D. (2013). Supportive supervisors and managerial coaching: exploring their intersections, *Journal of Occupational and Organizational Psychology*, 86(3): 310–16.

Engelbrecht, A.S., Heine, G. and Mahembe, B. (2014). The influence of ethical leadership on trust and work engagement: an exploratory study, *SA Journal of Industrial Psychology*, 40(1): article 2010. https://doi.org/10.4102/sajip.v40i1.1210.

Erkutlu, H. (2012). Impact of organisational culture on the relationship between shared leadership and team proactivity, *Team Performance Management: An International Journal*, 18(1/2): 102–19.

Fairhurst, G. and Connaughton, S.L. (2014). Leadership: a communication perspective, *Leadership*, 10(1): 7–35. DOI: 10.1177/1742715013509396.

Grint, K. (2010). *Leadership: A Very Short Introduction*. Oxford: Oxford University Press.

Grint, K. (2012). Leadership: a very short introduction, *Strategic Direction*, 28(10). https://doi.org/10.1108/sd.2012.05628jaa.003.

Hentschel, T., Shemla, M., Wegge, J. and Kearney, E. (2013). Perceived diversity and team functioning: the role of diversity beliefs and affect, *Small Group Research*, 44(1): 33–61.

Hinsz, V.B. (2015). Teams as technology: strengths, weaknesses, and trade-offs in cognitive task performance, *Team Performance Management*, 21(5/6): 218–30. DOI: 10.1108/TPM-02-2015-0006.

Hyland, C. (2013). Think, feel, know, *Training Journal*, July: 35–9.

Karaçivi, A. and Demirel, A. (2014). A futuristic commentary: coach-like leadership, *International Journal of Business and Social Science*, 5(9): 126–33.

Kegan, R. (1998). *In Over Our Heads: The Mental Demands of Modern Life*. Cambridge, MA: Harvard University Press.

Kim, S. (2014). Assessing the influence of managerial coaching on employee outcomes, *Human Resource Development Quarterly*, 25(1): 59–85.

Kunnanatt, J.T. (2016). 3D leadership – strategy-linked leadership framework for managing teams, *Economics, Management, and Financial Markets*, 11(3): 30–55.

Lin, W. (2015). Leading future orientations for current effectiveness: the role of engagement and supervisor coaching in linking future work self-salience to job performance, *Journal of Vocational Behavior*, 92: 145–56.

Maruping, L.M., Viswanath, V. and Thatcher, S.M. (2015). Folding under pressure or rising to the occasion? Perceived time pressure and the moderating role of team temporal leadership, *Academy of Management Journal*, 58(5): 1313–33.

Nielsen, K. and Randall, R. (2012). The importance of employee participation and perceptions of changes in a teamwork intervention, *Work & Stress*, 26(2): 91–111.

Norreklit, H. (2011). The art of managing individuality, *Qualitative Research in Accounting & Management*, 8(3): 265–91.

Oktug, Z. (2013). Managing emotions in the workplace: its mediating effect on the relationship between organizational trust and occupational stress, *International Business Research*, 6(4): 81–8.

Paustain-Underdahl, S.C., Shanock, L.R. and Rogelberg, S.G. (2013). Antecedents to supportive supervision: an examination of biographical data, *Journal of Occupational and Organizational Psychology*, 86(3): 288–309.

Peng, J.C. and Lin, J. (2016). Linking supervisor feedback environment to contextual performances: the mediating effect of leader–member exchange, *Leadership & Organization Development Journal*, 37(6): 802–20.

Peters, J. and Carr, C. (2013). Team effectiveness and team coaching literature review, *Coaching: An International Journal of Theory, Research and Practice*, 6(2): 116–36. DOI: 10.1080/17521882.2013.798669.

Pulakos, E.D., Hanson, L.M., Arad, S. and Moye, N. (2015). Performance management can be fixed: an on-the-job experiential learning approach for complex behaviour change, *Industrial and Organizational Psychology: Perspectives on Science and Practice*, 8: 51–76.

Rutti, R.M., Ramsey, J.R. and Chenwei, L. (2012). The role of other orientation in team selection and anticipated performance, *Team Performance Management: An International Journal*, 18(1/2): 41–58.

Santos, C.M. and Passos, A.M. (2013). Team mental models, relationship conflict and effectiveness over time, *Team Performance Management*, 19(7/8): 363–85.

Sommers, C. (2012). *Think Like a Futurist: Know What Changes, What Doesn't, and What's Next*. San Francisco, CA: John Wiley & Sons.

Tuckman, B.W. (1965). Developmental sequence in small groups, *Psychological Bulletin*, 65(6): 384–99.

Wageman, R., Gardener, H. and Mortensen, M. (2012). The changing ecology of teams: new directions for research teams, *Journal of Organizational Behaviour*, 33(33): 301–15.

Wiedow, A. and Konradt, U. (2011). Two dimensional structure of team process improvement: team reflection and team adaption, *Small Group Work*, 42(1): 32–54. DOI: 10.1177/1046496410377358.

Wilson, J.L. (2007). Virtual teaming: placing preservice middle level teachers on interdisciplinary teams, *Research in Middle Level Education Online*, 31(3): 1–15.

Wood, S., Michaelides, G. and Thomson, C. (2011). Team approach, idea generation, conflict and performance, *Team Performance Management: An International Journal*, 17(7/8): 382–404. http://dx.doi.org/10.1108/13527591111182643.

Zoltan, R. (2015). Group dynamics and team functioning in an organisational context, *Ecoforum*, 4(2): 154–8.

Psychology references

Deci, E.L. and Ryan, R.M. (1980). The empirical exploration of intrinsic motivational processes, in L. Berkowitz (ed.) *Advances in Experimental Social Psychology*, vol. 13. New York: Academic Press, pp. 39–80.

Sheldon, K.M. and Elliot, A.J. (1998). Not all personal goals are personal: comparing autonomous and controlled reasons for goals as predictors of effort and attainment, *Personality and Social Psychology Bulletin*, 24(5): 546–57.

2 Team context

Summary

This chapter highlights how current environmental demands make team challenge an even more pressing issue to understand, appreciate and manage. Imposed changes outside of our control impact internal team functioning and are commonplace factors which leaders, managers and team members need to accommodate to ensure continued functioning of the team and delivery of common objectives.

Keywords: resource scarcity, employee demands, team configuration

Introduction

Context is all important. We have lived through immense change in recent years due to a global pandemic affecting every aspect of how we function. We bear witness to how an unavoidable environmental change can have far-reaching impact on our lives. This can be further realized in a team context, when a single incident can bring about a change of circumstance, planned or not. Modern society is described as volatile, uncertain, complex and ambiguous – or VUCA (Bennis et al. 1985). Certainly we can all appreciate this first-hand, having lived through a pandemic, while in a team context dealing with issues that consistently impact on peak performance at an individual, team and organizational level is a primary consideration of any modern manager or leader.

Aims

Being alert to the elements that have an impact on the team context is an essential monitoring role for the manager or leader to be aware of and to check regularly. Setting the correct context (Dexter 2010) and influencing the desired course of action (Amos and Klimoski 2014) are essential if a team is to achieve its required goals. Fillery-Travis and Cavicchia (2013) describe this required functional context within a team as the complementarity of working alliances. This chapter aims to outline the items every manager or leader should be aware of, as highlighted by the managers interviewed. Their background encompassed a wide variety of sectors such as public, private, armed forces and voluntary, from SMEs (small to medium-sized enterprises) to large corporations. Their experience and feedback offered significant credibility in the choice of contextual challenges and universal acceptance.

Resource scarcity

Aligned with increasing complexity, there has been a move towards flatter, more flexible structures within organizations. Teams are now increasingly experiencing such changes (Dexter 2010; Amos and Klimoski 2014) which in many cases demand higher achievement and attainment levels with less resource. As an example, consider the constraints on the NHS during the pandemic: a shortage of PPE (personal protective equipment); increasing numbers of daily admissions (patients); lowering staff levels through sickness, stress, tiredness, overwork, back-to-back shifts and no leave allowed during the height of the outbreak. The challenge of *lack of time* as a resource, as discussed earlier, was also considered acute. In addition, the pandemic was subject to a perfect storm in terms of resource scarcity, with an estimated 46,000–50,000 shortfall in nursing staff and the inability of the health authorities to address this speedily due to Brexit employment regulations, plus a challenging time constraint to examine, recruit and train new nursing applicants.

VUCA changes impact team dynamics and can be attributed to the contemporary nature of the workplace and an increasingly complex and interconnected environment. The move towards flatter management structures has been driven by the need to make more rapid decisions, potentially saving time through removal of red tape, seizing opportunities and being more reactive to daily demands. In addition, for some sectors the need to remove an expensive layer of employees (middle managers) for financial reasons results from implementation of leaner management restructuring. This often arises from mergers or acquisitions, which have become commonplace in many sectors. Devolving management leads to team members becoming increasingly responsible through consultation and the need to function effectively. Supporting this rapid change in team structure and responsibility is the contribution to and from the constantly evolving technological landscape, impacting on tools, platform applications, processes and systems, while teams are frequently structured around solving complex problems within organizations (Borek 2011). As a result, teams may often be pulled together to address and focus on one specific output task, for example the development and launch of a new product which, once completed, results in the disbanding of the team.

The timeline of team tasks that these individuals are contributing towards can also vary in duration as well as complexity, adding another layer of demand and potential scarcity on the availability of individuals in the team. Individuals with the required skills can be the scarcity in some sectors and situations; employees that are flexible enough to accommodate such change and still be willing to engage are valuable indeed. This changing context could be argued to have turned the tables in favour of these skilled and agile workers, realizing their own value and thus playing to the scarcity in the market, and as a result being in a position to call the shots.

Employee demands

To deliver within a VUCA organizational scenario is demanding, and achieving the desired output requires agility and flexibility from each team member. They need to rapidly absorb and integrate different sources of information and apply their expertise to cope with the increased complexity and demands to deliver the team's purpose. This sequencing and synchronizing of the activities of individuals in the team is an essential requirement of a fully functioning team. In such a context, it can be appreciated how individual team members can offer competitive advantage to a team and organization if they are very agile and highly skilled. These individuals may be required to move around frequently to apply their unique skills or expertise to facilitate specific projects that require their input, possibly across several project teams simultaneously, even across organizations and multiple geographic locations. This mobile way of working also demands a flatter structure, as referenced earlier, to enable agile movement and flexibility, along with the potential that such individuals may not report to one manager or project leader, but multiple project leads, all with varying timelines. In such an ever-changing environment the ability to work at pace and under pressure may be a commonplace requirement, but it will have an impact on achieving the team and ultimately organizational objectives. The post-pandemic employee landscape has changed, with many employees reassessing their work integration, considering the possibility of home working and potentially reducing the number of days worked each week. This adds to the evaluation of how to meet these evolving employee demands while still creating a fully functioning team to achieve the desired organizational goals.

Successful goal execution is only realized if the team members can task-manage effectively to facilitate their interdependent tasks cohesively. This requires coordination and cooperation from each team member. Coordination needs clarity. For this clarity to be acted upon, team members must have an appreciation of the wider context to offer purpose to their individual task and their contribution to the whole. Teamwork is therefore an adaptive, dynamic and episodic process that encompasses thoughts, feelings and behaviours among team members while interacting towards shared common goals. To facilitate the wider context of how appreciation and interactive contribution can be embedded within the team, there must also be a social connection with fellow team members to engage fully, even if those team members are demographically distant from one another. Demographic change and increased globalization have created a wider pool of employees, which has added diversity.

While diversity is a positive development, it can also present a further challenging context to be considered and accommodated within a team. Negatively perceived diversity by any team member can influence individual team member identification and create relationship conflict (Peng and Lin 2016), leading to a potential impact on team performance. Other negative effects of non-diversity acceptance could be decreases in areas such as creativity, which will likely curtail the team's ability to be agile through evolving creative solutions as required; or increased group think, diminished communication, inhibited social integration and a reluctance to share, which could potentially cause increased staff turnover (Engelbrecht et al. 2014) through not feeling accepted, included, valued or encouraged to engage. Ultimately this leads to marginalized individuals not feeling accepted or belonging to the team, thereby hampering their ability to engage fully, and being frustrated at not being fully utilized. This can lead to a decision to leave the organization.

Staff turnover is expensive and does not contribute to achieving team outputs efficiently; neither does it build a strong or positive reputation for the organization as being a desirable place to work. If this trend is confined to a specific team, we may be wondering what is wrong with that team environment. Appreciative working alliances need to be forged between team members through positive perceptions of each other's diversity, which can result in an improved working environment, retaining staff through a feeling of belonging, as well as providing increased competitive advantage for the team and the organization through sharing knowledge and ideas generation. These issues can enhance collective team learning and improve decision-making. Another researcher, Edmondson (who we shall revisit later), also confirmed the link between the establishment of positive relationships, team learning behaviour and team performance (Edmondson 2012). Positively performing teams entice other employees to want to join that team, especially those who view work as a means of self-development and learning. These individuals are not wrong since we know teams are considered to be conduits for information sharing, reflective communication and exchange interactions between team members, resulting in personal changes in cognition, behaviour and performance (Hentschel et al. 2013). A fully functioning team can have a contagion impact beyond the team itself. For example, think of the Nobel Prize-winning teams and what they can achieve through sharing knowledge, collaboration and communicating effectively, both inside and outside the team, or even the team's parent organization.

Individual team member behaviour is a pivotal element in setting the required team context and its impact on other team members in a positive or negative sense. Factors such as fairness in the workplace can have a positive reward or a negative threatening consequence that influences work-related attitudes and behaviours (Hall 2013: 4). Positive social exchange can lead to improved employee performance (Al-Nasser and Mohamed 2015). The link between the establishment of positive relationships, team learning behaviour and team performance is well documented (Edmondson 1999, cited in Savelsbergh et al. 2010). Behavioural modelling highlighting the expected actions of organizational members is a powerful influence on all team members, and as a result team context, setting standards within and for the team.

Such intra-team behaviour can influence the emotional state of each employee within the team and their potential job performance. Our feelings, moods and emotions impact not only ourselves but also those around us, whatever our position or role is within the team. Negative attitudes cause employees to exhibit negative work behaviours (Peng and Lin 2016). As adult learning is highly influenced by observation (Rutti et al. 2012; Sun et al. 2017), we can appreciate that the behaviours displayed within a team set the standard and ultimately the team culture. Consider the scenario where it is common practice for team members to help themselves to the office supplies and take them home. This could be establishing theft as an acceptable standard, so when a new team member joins the team and observes others in the team doing this, how can we expect them to do otherwise? Thus, the way individuals across the whole team behave can affect the desired learning of individual team members, impacting individual and team performance, standards and effectiveness (Yang et al. 2015; Peng and Lin 2016).

Since human beings are social creatures, the importance of each individual within a team when investigating team influence through social sharing stresses that team members not only amplify positive emotions but can also mitigate negative emotions. Team members develop new insights into the appropriate and accepted attitudes and behaviours at work by comparing the consequences of their own behaviour and actions to that of their colleagues. Eventually, a new constructive meaning can be formed through this observational lens and learning from colleagues, bringing about a reinterpretation of each experience, thus evolving the accepted performance and standards for that team. Assuming the displayed behaviours and intra-team sharing is positive, it is imperative for the correct communication, standards and context to be created to enable a fully functional team.

Team members that are open to sharing and understanding the skills and knowledge of their colleagues evolve positive patterns of behaviour and an appreciative attitude towards the key elements of a task. This can affect the anticipated needs and actions of the team in being proactive and therefore improving its ability to function effectively (Santos and Passos 2013). Where open learning and sharing is the normal team context, improved collective performance can result. The flow of work between team members becomes seamless, enabling increased efficiency and resultant output. This intra-team sharing allows team members to appreciate each other's contribution to the team, which enhances sequencing and synchronizing configurations. This understanding also means individuals can step up and cover or assist a colleague as demands require.

Team configuration

This dynamic team context consists of all the interdependent elements of the social self, including personal value systems, all of which can affect one's mindset. This mindset is responsible for our perception of others. In psychological terms, the required alignment of mindset within a team is referred to as mental closeness (Forsyth 2010, cited in Zoltan 2015). Achieving this positive mental closeness or shared mindset is essential to evolve a fully synchronized configuration for an optimally functioning team. This appreciation of the importance of mindset shines a spotlight on the importance of individual behaviour when observing that an attitude represents an evaluative disposition (mindset) towards a certain situation, object or person. This mindset disposition can hold great sway over our perception and relationship outcomes with others in the team – negatively or positively. Individuals with a positive attitude and mindset are more likely to behave consistently and aligned with that attitude (Agarwal et al. 2009) and impact individuals and the team accordingly. These same team members tend to be proactively self-directed, flexible, versatile and driven by personal values, highly satisfied with their work and are less likely to be affected by uncertainty and more able to collaborate with other team members (Auer et al. 2014). This positive attitude within the team can lead to a shared psychological state or mindset alignment, resulting in collective commitment through the feelings of loyalty and a desire to invest mentally and physically in achieving the team and organizational goals (Conway and Coyle-Shapiro 2012). This is evidence of positive mental closeness. Such proactive positive behaviour is also related to organizational citizenship and a willingness to support and assist other team members, fostering a positive social infrastructure within a team and organization where workers feel energized and able to engage. Committed employees are likely to engage in proactive pro-organizational behaviour, and employees who are committed to their team engage in proactive interpersonal behaviour (Maruping et al. 2015), thereby impacting the positive atmosphere of the whole team. This positive context acts as a fuel for increasing commitment to a specific team, leading to an increase in functional behaviour and furthering the success of that team (Belschak and Den Hartog 2010). It becomes an enduring cycle.

Several enabling mechanisms of a functioning team are at play simultaneously, such as communication, coordination and cooperation, which help team members improve their work tasks and relational interactions (Ehrhardt et al. 2013). Configuring this interdependent team architecture for peak functioning is essential for any team. Successful goal execution is only realized if the team can task-manage effectively and facilitate interdependent activities cohesively (Santos and Passos 2013). Achieving this successful cohesion requires an ability to coordinate tasks by all team members, which requires optimum team configuration (all playing to our strengths) or complementarity of working alliances. However, if any of the aforementioned enabling mechanisms are impeded or missing, the functional team configuration process becomes a dysfunctional process configuration. This dysfunctional configuration or behaviour could be applied to any person, process or system at any point in the life cycle of a task or team working, underlining the requirement for a continuous open communication flow, seamless coordination and open cooperation between team members. It is noted that teams do not think, feel or behave, but individuals that make up those teams do (Kozlowski and Bell 2008), making the creation of a conducive context for peak performance even more complex. This aspect is even more vital in the modern VUCA team for individuals to engage, contribute and participate fully. If you have ever worked in a peak-performing team, you will know it is worth the effort to create such a context, and if achieved, results can far exceed expectations.

Underpinning considerations

Social cognitive and self-regulation theories

Albert Bandura is the founding father of this particular field of psychological appreciation and the theories that provide an explanation to support effective teaming from the perspective of social cognitive theory. Human beings are social creatures and influenced by our social and physical environment, our own personal state (both physically and mentally) and the individuals we engage with such as team members and team managers or leaders, who collectively can impact our behaviour.

Bandura (2001) postulates that social cognitive theory is *an agentic perspective to self-development, adaption and change*. Bandura explains there are four elements to social cognitive theory that bring about efficacy in an individual: 1) mastery experience, founded on past successful experiences (and observations) building confidence in one's own ability or facilitating self-regulatory change if not successful; 2) the variety of experiences available to the individual through social models being observed in other established team members, especially where the team culture (*how we do things here*) may offer specific social models; 3) verbal persuasion and other social influences from the team members, e.g. cheering on, anecdotal feedback on their performance etc.; and 4) the individual's own psychological and emotional state, which can impact on their vision of their own ability to succeed or not, as per the famous line *if you believe you can – you can*.

With this explanation, we can appreciate how team members may adapt to influence one another positively or negatively. As a team manager or leader we may witness how a newly recruited individual fits into the team, interacts and develops relationships within the team in addition to how the team changes over time with a new team member. Forging a positive relationship with the new team member may diminish other relationships in the team. The dynamics of the team will change with the incoming of one new member, changing how all individuals react to one another until they know the new recruit, and assess how they fit in and complement other team members' existing skills and knowledge. Once established, a new way of working and team dynamic is possible. The same jostling for position happens when an established team members leaves.

We learn from infancy that our actions result in various outcomes that affect our thoughts, feelings and behaviour; consider how a baby learns that if they cry, they may get attention and be picked up and cuddled. This leads to self-regulation of this behaviour on the part of the baby. This is the same model of self-regulation that plays out in a team; individuals within the team may set themselves goals, anticipating the likely outcome, which guides their actions to achieve that goal, motivating their effort (especially where there may be a reward attached) to attain the set goals via self-regulation. This self-regulation is referred to as self-efficacy when we realize how our personal performance can impact output. If this output is required as part of a team task, engagement through *wanting* to achieve the team task is essential. As team leaders and managers, we may exploit this self-regulation with individual team members by offering rewards and enticements to motivate further performance. It is important to realize that we cannot entice all employees in the same way as not all are motivated by similar things – for example, flexi-time, time in lieu or extra pay in lieu of time worked are issues which may be more valuable to some vs. others in the team.

Case study – team context

Sallie was an experienced and sensitive teacher but decided on a career change in her mid-30s to join a sales team in an organization that played to her teaching knowledge and background. She felt comfortable about this change and was looking forward to meeting her colleagues and team members on completing the initial training course and induction. Sallie did really well in her scores in the training as well as later in practice in her allocated territory and won many accolades for her achievements in this job. Sadly, after a couple of years she handed in her notice due to her partner's career move, a cause of great sadness for Sallie at the time.

Having established a good reputation with this organization it wasn't too surprising that Sallie had a phone call one day about 18 months later from her previous line manager when a vacancy came up in the area she had moved to. Wow, perfect one would think, and no need to go on the training course again, just hit the road running, a dream for the employer and for Sallie. The usual paperwork was addressed; Sallie could even pick up where her previous pension contributions had been and gained a slight increase in salary.

Since this was a different area of the country this meant Sallie was part of a different region and a different team, plus she was assigned to a new line manager. This manager had been informed by Sallie's previous line manager of her arrival and her successful history, and the scene was set to make a fabulous contribution to an organization and role Sallie loved. That was the first assumption Sallie made.

The new line manager was not best pleased that he had been told he was being assigned Sallie as a team member: someone he had not chosen, not interviewed or approved of independently. Things did not get off to a great start and Sallie was always picked out in team meetings by the line manager with comments such as 'Sallie should know, she's experienced!' This may not have been too awkward or bad to tolerate, but the line manager did this openly and garnered support from team members. This put Sallie's colleagues in an awkward situation; should they be loyal and supportive to a fellow team member or to their line manager? In addition, the manner of the line manager was making many of the team members unsure of Sallie due to inappropriate jibes and comments. More importantly, this impacted on the general atmosphere in the team, who felt threatened by this person who had been part of a rival team.

In this situation, the line manager had a massive impact on the context of the team by not setting a positive work environment and fostering positive mental closeness between the team members. No team introductions were carried out to facilitate an appreciation of each team member's contribution to the team, while not setting a platform for sharing or open communication. The line manager was more concerned with their own agenda as opposed to the requirement of the team in building a healthy positive environment. Even though this was a fabulous opportunity for Sallie, the organization and the line manager concerned, the relationship went sour and after a year Sallie was poached by a rival organization for a promotional position. Sallie left.

There are seldom winners by not creating a positive team context (except the rival organization that hired Sallie). A positive working environment works for all team members including line managers. Sadly this line manager failed to realize that embracing Sallie could have done him and the team good – they all could have benefitted from her experience and work ethic. But instead they lagged behind other teams through having another vacancy to be filled on the same territory again, hampering confidence from the client base and leaving opportunities open to competitors.

Reflective questions

- What are the areas of resource scarcity in my teams? What sorts of tensions do I observe these creating in my teams? Which are those I cannot control, and which are the ones I can influence?
- How have I (or someone else) set up my teams – how would I describe their team design? To what extent is there separation or overlap in roles or responsibilities and what is the intention of that?
- How do my teams coordinate themselves? Is there clarity and shared buy-in to this? What are the vulnerabilities of this approach?
- How effective is communication within and across my teams? What evidence do I have to confirm (or disconfirm) this?
- As a manager/leader, how have I previously encouraged engagement of my team members? What have I observed working – or not? What did that tell my about how the team is configured or what the team needs?

- To what extent are there individuals in my teams that may have an issue with self-regulation? How do I know this – what evidence do I have?
- Once I make an intervention in any of the above areas, how will I know things have changed?

References

Agarwal, R., Angst, C.M. and Magni, M. (2009). The performance effects of coaching: a multilevel analysis using hierarchical linear modelling, *International Journal of Human Resource Management*, 20(10): 2110–34. DOI: 10.1080/09585190903178054.

Al-Nasser, A. and Mohamed, B. (2015). Examining the relationship between organizational coaching and workplace counterproductive behaviours in the United Arab Emirates, *International Journal of Organizational Analysis*, 23(3): 378–403. DOI: 10.1108/IJOA-08-2014-0793.

Amos, B. and Klimoski, R.J. (2014). Courage: making teamwork work well, *Group & Organization Management*, 39(1): 110–28. DOI: 10.1177/1059601113520407.

Auer, J.C., Kao, C.-Y., Hemphill, L., Johnston, E.W. and Teasley, S.D. (2014). The uncertainty challenge of contingent collaboration, *Human Resource Management Journal*, 24(4): 531–47.

Belschak, F.D. and Den Hartog, D.N. (2010). Pro-self, pro-social, and pro-organizational foci of proactive behaviour: differential antecedents and consequences, *Journal of Occupational and Organizational Psychology*, 83(2): 475–98.

Bennis, W.G., Nanus, B. and Bennis, S. (1985). *Leaders: Strategies for Taking Charge*, vol. 200. New York: Harper & Row.

Borek, L. (2011). Team structural constellations and intra-team conflict, *Team Performance Management: An International Journal*, 17(7/8): 405–17. http://dx.doi.org/10.1108/13527591111182652.

Conway, N. and Coyle-Shapiro, J.A.M. (2012). The reciprocal relationship between psychological contract fulfilment and employee performance and the moderating role of perceived organisational support and tenure, *Journal of Occupational and Organizational Psychology*, 85(2): 277–99.

Dexter, B. (2010). Critical success factors for developmental team projects, *Team Performance Management: An International Journal*, 16(7/8): 343–58. http://dx.doi.org/10.1108/13527591011090637.

Ehrhardt, K., Miller, J.S., Freeman, S.J. and Hom, P.W. (2013). Examining project commitment in cross-functional teams: antecedents and relationship with team performance, *Journal of Business and Psychology*, 29(3): 443–61. DOI: 10.1007/s10869-013-9325.

Engelbrecht, A.S., Heine, G. and Mahembe, B. (2014). The influence of ethical leadership on trust and work engagement: an exploratory study, *SA Journal of Industrial Psychology*, 40(1): article 2010. https://doi.org/10.4102/sajip.v40i1.1210.

Fillery-Travis, A. and Cavicchia, S. (2013). Coaching at work – a method of facilitating self-directed learning or controlling it?, in *Researching Work and Learning: The Visible and Invisible in Work and Learning* [conference proceedings], June 2013, Sterling University.

Hall, J.L. (2013). Managing teams with diverse compositions: implications for managers from research on the faultline model, *Advanced Management Journal*, 78(1): 4–10.

Hentschel, T., Shemla, M., Wegge, J. and Kearney, E. (2013). Perceived diversity and team functioning: the role of diversity beliefs and affect, *Small Group Research*, 44(1): 33–61.

Kozlowski, S.W.J. and Bell, B.S. (2008). Team learning, development, and adaptation, in V.I. Sessa and M. London (eds), *Work Group Learning: Understanding, Improving and Assessing How Groups Learn in Organizations*. New York: Taylor & Francis, pp. 15–44.

Maruping, L.M., Viswanath, V. and Thatcher, S.M. (2015). Folding under pressure or rising to the occasion? Perceived time pressure and the moderating role of team temporal leadership, *Academy of Management Journal*, 58(5): 1313–33.

Peng, J.C. and Lin, J. (2016). Linking supervisor feedback environment to contextual performances: the mediating effect of leader–member exchange, *Leadership & Organization Development Journal*, 37(6): 802–20.

Rutti, R.M., Ramsey, J.R. and Chenwei, L. (2012). The role of other orientation in team selection and anticipated performance, *Team Performance Management: An International Journal*, 18(1/2): 41–58.

Santos, C.M. and Passos, A.M. (2013). Team mental models, relationship conflict and effectiveness over time, *Team Performance Management*, 19(7/8): 363–85.

Savelsbergh, C.M.J.H., van der Heijden, B.I.J.M. and Poell, R.F. (2010). Attitudes towards factors influencing team performance, *Team Performance Management: An International Journal*, 16(7/8): 451–74. http://dx.doi.org/10.1108/13527591011090682.

Sun, H., Pei-Lee, T. and Karis, H. (2017). Team diversity, learning, and innovation: a mediation model, *Journal of Computer Information Systems*, 57(1): 22–30.

Yang, M.-Y., Cheng, F.-C. and Chuang, A. (2015). The role of affects in conflict frames and conflict management, *International Journal of Conflict Management*, 26(4): 427–49.

Zoltan, R. (2015). Group dynamics and team functioning in an organisational context, *Ecoforum*, 4(2): 154–8.

Psychology reference

Bandura, A. (2001). Social cognitive theory: an agentic perspective, *Annual Review of Psychology*, 52: 1–26.

3 Understanding team effectiveness

Summary

This chapter reviews current established and respected models for team effectiveness and academic literature on the subject to provide the reader with a solid platform for understanding what is defined as team effectiveness. We appreciate that effectiveness is a subjective measure, and may vary from team to team and business to business. Regardless of our measure, there are some universally accepted items we can address as leaders and managers that will facilitate any team to be more effective. The chapter considers these enablers from the established and lived experience viewpoints, allowing an insight into areas for potential improvement in context.

Keywords: team effectiveness, enabling structures – cohesion, sharing, safe environment, clarity of direction, interpersonal focus

Introduction

This chapter looks at some of the current established models for team effectiveness and reviews the supportive literature to offer an understanding of how team effectiveness can be defined. So, what does effectiveness mean in a team context? Fleishman (1992), Katzenbach and Smith (1999), Hackman (2002) and Edmondson (2012), as a small sample of the team models available, all identify specific requirements for successful team functioning – team effectiveness elements which are still relevant in a constantly changing team. A summary analysis of these team effectiveness models is presented in Table 3.1.

Since teams are composed of unique individuals, engaging these individuals to work collectively as a single entity is essential to the effective functioning of a team. The effectiveness of a team is understandably reliant on multiple levels of individual personal engagement. Team members need to work at a micro level with one another to create a conducive environment for cooperation and coordination to flourish. This cooperation is often described as being facilitated by socio-cognition (Agrawal 2012), implying that each team member needs to be physically and (especially) mentally social towards their work colleagues, and have no barriers that could inhibit an acceptance of their work colleagues, thereby enabling an effective working relationship via mental alignment and closeness.

Table 3.1 Comparison and summary of team effectiveness models

Fleishman Team leadership framework 1992	Katzenbach & Smith Team basics model 1999	Hackman Real team effectiveness 2002	Edmondson in Ghosh et al. Team EI and effect upon team learning 2012	Summary of team effectiveness models
enabling structure task-focused	accountability commitment and skills	enabling structure to facilitate a *real team*	team members trust in team environment	**trust accountability commitment (enabling structures)**
supportive organizational context task-focused	mutual accountability, small number of people, individual	supportive organizational context overarching all team activities	team members feel *safe* with one another.	**organizational support for individuals and teams creating a safe environment**
compelling direction personal focus	specific goal meaningful purpose, common approach	compelling direction	work environment perceived as *safe* impacts performance through freeing members to focus on outputs	**clarity of direction meaningful purpose minimize distractions focus on goals**
expert coaching person-focused task-focused	skills – interpersonal, technical and problem-solving	expert coaching underpinning all team activities	EI within team members increases ability to manage emotions, build trust and team learning	**coaching interpersonal focus problem-solving enhanced learning**
increased capacity both in leadership and team output when material resources are managed	personal growth, collective work products, performance results	team effectiveness measure through outputs	building trust within work environment ask questions seek feedback reflect and discuss unexpected outcomes of actions or errors	**effectiveness of collaborative teamwork trusted environment**
outputs perceived effectiveness, team productivity team learning	performance results	outputs such as product acceptability to clients growth of team capability and individual learning	increased stability (EI) trust, improved learning team outputs	**perceived outcomes improved learning and capabilities**

Aims

All the respected authors listed in Table 3.1 mention *enabling structures* as being things such as *trust, accountability and commitment to the team activities*, and if present these structures can result in a safe team environment, creating clarity and meaningful purpose to the team tasks, facilitating engagement, collaboration and improved working capabilities. What team leader would not want to foster these characteristics in their team to achieve the peak team effectiveness possible? This chapter aims to review the elements that a team leader or manager needs to be aware of and how to establish them as enablers within their team.

Enabling structures

From the comparison of four chosen team effectiveness models in Table 3.1, reference to an enabling structure by Fleishman and Hackman is the first area for further exploration. Enabling structures can refer to the physical, mental or process structures, availability and quality of resources, appropriateness of equipment and materials, along with the individual team member's ability and skills being made available to carry out the task required, thus enabling the achievement of the whole team activity. Some of the enabling structures referred to may include clear communication, cooperation and coordination between team members, as mentioned in Chapter 2. Absence of any one of these enabling structures can obstruct the team in achieving its shared output.

Hackman's explanation of enabling structures brings about a status that he describes as a *real team*. If you have ever been fortunate enough to be part of a really great team, you may be able to reminisce as to why it felt so great, what you think made it work, what made it a success, how team members interacted with one another and so forth. I am sure you can recall the way that team environment made you feel even now, and you may be able to remember specific processes and systems adopted within the team to enable it to function as well as it did. When we can recall such team experiences, we are likely having little glimpses of what makes a truly efficient, enabled team. Thus, we can appreciate some of the elements Fleishman and Hackman are referring to. Sadly, as human beings we seem to be able to vividly recall the negatives more than the positive aspects from an experience, due to our neurological (fright, fight or flight) wiring that alerts us to any scenario that may cause us harm. In the case of efficient, enabled team working this is equally as valuable a recollection though, offering us a blueprint of what not to aspire to in a team, what not to do to create a *real team*, what does not work as an enabling structure so may need to be changed, and what does not build a conducive environment to operate efficiently within a team. Maybe you have had such experiences too, offering a good guide for what to avoid. A major element that is often reported by those who have experienced a great team experience say they felt safe, and there was nothing that held them back in the team environment that could inhibit performance. A safe team environment is our next enabling focus.

Safe team environment

What makes a safe environment for anyone? We are not just referring solely to the physical environment here but also the psychological environment. The needs of one employee vs. another can be vastly different to elicit from them the best possible contribution to the team. You may have come across something referred to as Herzberg's hygiene factors (Herzberg et al. 1959). Herzberg suggested there were certain factors that made an environment appealing to some employees and not to others, that could influence their chosen workplace. The elements that can be dissatisfiers according to Herzberg that would not make a company or team a particularly appealing or 'safe' place to work for some employees are listed as: management style, company policies, pay and status, job security, working conditions and interpersonal relationships. The motivational elements of Herzberg's hygiene factors are challenge, achievement, responsibility, recognition, advancement and growth.

Considering the various elements of an enabling structure, other authors from Table 3.1 such as Katzenbach and Smith and Edmondson focus on *team basics*, such as possessing the right skills and the emotional intelligence of the individual team members to enable team functioning. These elements are noted as being key to an enabling structure. Edmondson's reference to each team member trusting in the team environment is akin to that referred to by Herzberg and Katzenbach and Smith highlighting the need for team members to be accountable to each other for their actions within the team. In combination with Edmondson's focus on emotional intelligence, it can be appreciated how complex these various layers of the team environment may be. If one individual in a team does not commit to the team activities or is not willing to be accountable for their actions within the team, how can other team members trust this team member, and therefore how can the subsequent team environment be conducive to peak performance? Edmondson specifically mentioned the need for team members to *feel safe with one another* to enable a fully functioning team.

The team environment is highlighted again by Edmondson at an organizational level through supporting individuals to achieve the team activities and thus allowing them to feel safe in the activities they need to perform. This feeling of safety could be something as simple as being sponsored by the organization for correct training to acquire the right skills to contribute to a specific team task. The *feeling safe* factor could be having the right equipment to do your job, feeling safe in the team environment, feeling safe working with these colleagues, or feeling safe in the knowledge you are doing the right thing because you have the correct skills. All of these cooperative factors are therefore reliant on multiple elements to build this feeling of safety. From a manager or leader viewpoint, it is about the explicit application of knowing what activity is required and when, where and with whom in the team, that creates a safe environment for all, and showing faith and confidence in your colleagues to deliver.

The importance of any one of the factors listed can be different for each team member depending on their personal circumstances. The hygiene factors mentioned can make the difference between an acceptable or rejected work environment for an individual, and will be of consideration when moving from one post to another, or via for example a pension package or earned additional annual leave acquired through long service. Therefore, the connections between these hygiene factors and an individual's motivation can be appreciated and are important for a line manager or leader to be aware of if they wish to avoid losing critical employees. The point where the employee is in their career trajectory will further impact their decision concerning these factors. Some hygiene factors can become more important than others at different stages in our career. Once all the hygiene and environmental factors are in place, the next item to consider in team motivation is the creation of a compelling direction.

Compelling direction

The third essential element for team effectiveness is essential to all the models summarized, even if expressed differently. That is clarification of focus: a clear, compelling direction and meaningful purpose. This is an important stage for any team to clarify and for its members to grasp, and has several steps in becoming a reality:

- An understanding of core values to describe the team's deeply held beliefs which feed into team purpose and mission – *something to believe in.*
- Clear purpose is a consequence of why a team exists and how that team impacts on the organization. If the team didn't exist, what would happen? – *something to align with.*
- A mission that describes what the team is trying to achieve – *something to connect with.*
- A strategy for how the team plans to realize the mission. Strategy can be long term – *something to focus on.*
- Goals that break down the strategy into shorter-term, achievable objectives and help align the team's efforts – *something to deliver and aspire to deliver.*

Together, the values, purpose, mission and strategies contribute to providing the team vision, a focus, a clear compelling direction and meaningful purpose as expressed in the chosen models. Basically, this is offering the rationale as to why the team exists, what the team is trying to achieve and how they will get there. This focus on *the goal* for team members minimizes distractions and as such enables a more efficient contribution from each team member, through knowing the task required and the purpose in its provision as a driver to deliver individually and for the whole team. Successful goal execution is only realized if the team can task-manage effectively and facilitate their interdependent tasks cohesively. To achieve this, each team member needs an appreciation of the overview and vision to align and hopefully connect with. Only then can they contribute correctly.

From the manager and leader interviews, there were several team challenges that related to undefined or poorly defined roles, and complex organizational structures. This resulted in the team members feeling disjointed and disconnected from the organizational purpose, i.e. they were missing the clear direction as listed by Fleishman, which led to compliance issues, errors and stress-related mistakes. Inefficient team functioning can develop into a dysfunctional team.

Interpersonal focus

The fourth element for efficient team functioning is related to the interpersonal relationships between team members. The responsibility for the smooth working and managing of team processes and team performance lies within the team itself (Herzberg 1966) and how they interact with one another, including the process of how they commit to sharing and working collaboratively together. Hence the focus from Edmondson in his model is on the emotional intelligence of each team member to facilitate team problem-solving and to foster learning from one another, allowing for increased team efficiency. This collaborative, open sharing atmosphere among the team will further offer opportunities to appreciate and build trust in one another's capabilities and hopefully create stronger bonds between team members. There has been much research on team cohesion and the elements that allow for this collaborative and cohesive state to be achieved. Cohesion is when team members *stick together* to achieve a joint objective or task (Amos and Klimoski 2014) regardless of the obstacles along the way, which understandably demands strong social connections between team members to make the team task possible.

There are four characteristics to establishing cohesion that can assist an appreciation of how complex it may be to achieve:

1 Cohesion is multidimensional – when different members come together to form a team.
2 Cohesion is dynamic – the VUCA context exerting pressure on the team, forcing change.
3 Cohesion is instrumental – supporting the clear purpose for the team working together.
4 Cohesion is affective – the development of social relationships during the team's existence.

These team cohesion characteristics echo the team effectiveness models in Table 3.1. Thus, achieving successful cohesion requires an ability to coordinate tasks for all team members, with coordination fostered through the creation of a positive, safe environment as discussed earlier. This safe environment provides an accepting, non-threatening platform for asking questions, enabling clarity of purpose and individual actions, seeking reassurance – all of which are considered constructive enablers of interpersonal connection within the team and with other team members. And, most importantly, allowing time for these interpersonal connections to be forged.

It is noteworthy that managers or leaders of project teams are advised to focus initially on task cohesion to enable collaboration and sharing, building and forming positive working relationships (Martin et al. 2013) and reinforcing the need for a compelling direction or focus to facilitate the desired collaborative context. An aligned joint purpose appears to be an essential platform for effective team activities to be made possible and is a feature which unifies and drives individuals within the team collectively towards their joint purpose. This fourth element of healthy interpersonal relationships is also underpinned by *expert coaching* according to the model by Hackman. This model will be revisited in Chapter 7.

Building healthy interpersonal relationships will enable the next important element of the team effectiveness models to be reviewed: that of fostering collaboration and trust among team members.

Collaboration and trust

While a willingness to complete the team task may be discretionary to some team members, the choice remains as to whether to engage or not as active participants in the work team and to collaborate or not. The outcome is impacted by whether we trust the colleagues we work alongside.

Collaborative teamwork has to be adaptive and dynamic. This is an episodic process that encompasses thoughts, feelings and behaviours among team members while interacting towards a common goal. Therefore, each team member's thoughts, feelings and behaviours can impact on the whole team output. If one team member is out of kilter, the whole team is affected. Our work mindset resulting from the thoughts, feelings and behaviours towards and from our teammates has been identified as having a potential impact on our wider work relationships (Gosling and Mintzberg 2003, cited in Laud et al. 2016).

This dynamic, episodic and adaptive team environment consists of all the interdependent elements of the social self, including value systems, which can affect the mindset of the individuals in the team. The more aligned the individuals become, the greater the team trust between colleagues. Further, collaboration is more likely if supported by a feeling of loyalty towards co-team workers, resulting in improved team functioning. Increased collaboration contributes towards increased commitment which in turn builds trust and increased proactivity between team colleagues. Proactive behaviour is related to organizational citizenship through increasing the desire to support and assist one's colleagues – a further facet of collaboration. Edmondson also notes that where the team achieves this level of collaboration, there is increased stability within the team (*reduced turnover*), increased trust and improved team learning and outputs. All these aspects positively contribute towards improved team functioning and the desired performance.

Perceived outcomes

The fifth essential element gleaned from the team effectiveness models is that of measuring and monitoring the desired outputs, seeking feedback, tracking progress and analysing results. Having such measures and metrics in place on an individual and team level increases the focus and potential for attaining the desired results, along with increased sharing and learning opportunities among team members. Setting standards to be aspired to and jointly achieving tasks can be motivational for individuals and the collective team. You will have heard of the statement *if it does not get measured it does not get done*. This could be true at one level through providing retrospective feedback individually and as a team on the performance level achieved and what quality standard is achieved and so forth. Due to increased emphasis being placed on the understanding of the team dynamics, such feedback outcomes can further act as a driving force for improved performance. The incorporation of efficient and appropriate measurement tools to understand how the individuals and the team perform over time becomes critical. The *over time* reference requires a shorter time frame to make reactions effective and corrective to prevent waste if measures do not align within required timelines, outputs and standards. Team members themselves need this immediate feedback loop, allowing them to take ownership and responsibility for corrective measures, as necessary.

As we have established, teams are not static. We require measurement and monitoring methods that are flexible and dynamic and potentially capture elements of the team environment, the safe feeling, and the cognitive sharing and growth, plus the appropriate raw metrics relating to specific outputs. The ability to measure the team's functional status as well as team outputs is the only way to glean a true representation of team performance on multiple levels. In addition, the feedback can be shared via open dialogue as a monitoring, checking-in function *as we go*. An assessment of team status in this manner can be seen as separate but linked to the next level of performance elements through offering a team leader or manager a window on the team at a functional level. This team functional status is described as the A-B-C of team dynamics (Buvik and Tvedt 2017), referring to the attitudes, shared behaviours and cognitions of the individuals that make up the team. This is sometimes referred to as the local team dynamics (Salas et al. 2015), highlighting how complex these layers and different elements of team functioning can be (as illustrated in Figure 3.1).

Figure 3.1 Elements of local team dynamics that impact team functionality

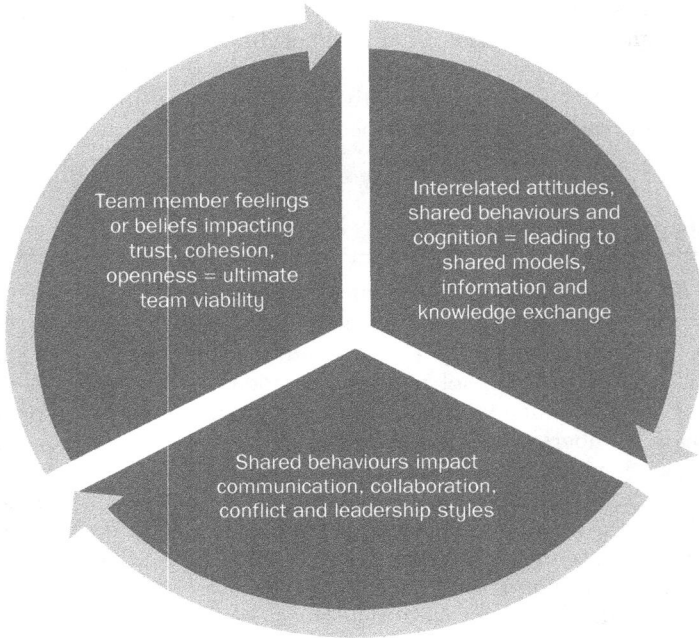

The cycle of team functioning and therefore performance potential will be impacted if any of these elements of local team dynamics are missing or out of alignment. An appreciation of how these elements and layers of team functioning bring a completely different insight to the interpretation of the forming, storming, norming and performing model has been suggested by Tuckman (1965) along with a heightened level of challenge for any team manager or leader wishing to support their team to be the best they possibly can be.

Performance quality and productivity

The final element for effective teams is that of performance quality and productivity from the perspective of the team, end users, individual capability, and growth and learning. We are aware that personal learning and growth experience is far more important to the younger generation and an important contributor to their job satisfaction criteria along with a desire for constant development to be specified in their job role. They want to feel they are progressing. They want to learn, and if they do not feel they are, they will be inclined to move elsewhere where they can achieve their requirements. Edmondson believes this is a cycle of learning and growth that can be delivered when the team becomes more stable, i.e. when the team is cohesive in its structure as discussed earlier. This cohesion facilitates growth and learning by and for the team members with greater freedom, thus enabling improved effectiveness and output. In general, cohesion is associated with group-level variables such as increased performance and collective efficacy as well as individual-level variables such as increased passion (displayed through engagement), satisfaction, return rate (of customers and employees) and decreased anxiety and depression of team members. Achieving this team state is essential for both team and individual performance. The individual-level variables of passion, satisfaction and decreasing anxiety and depression are very real items to be addressed, some even attenuated through the pandemic. If any team is to be effective in addressing these more personal well-being-focused issues, it is essential to care for our team members on a personal level. This is no longer an option and probably explains the recent noted increase in well-being associated with team functioning.

There are many models and publications concerning leading teams but the key themes listed by expert authors in Table 3.1 were endorsed and reinforced during the interviews with the present-day leaders and managers. These are regarded as the essential elements to be addressed, regardless of sector or context, in our quest to forge a fully functional team. If we operate within a knowledge exchange environment, which many of us do, team members will be accepting and open to learning about one another as a workable collaborative platform towards establishing team effectiveness. Teams really do rely on individuals.

Underpinning considerations

Self-determination theory

This theory is associated with the psychological value that team members ascribe to goals, their expectations regarding goal attainment and the mechanism that keeps them moving towards their selected goals. Self-determination theory differentiates the content of goals or outcomes and the regulatory processes to achieve those goals, which are linked to the individual needs to deliver that specific outcome: the means vs. the end result scenario.

Self-determination theory is described as a macro theory of human motivation, which means it is one of the essential motivations we possess which drives our personal development, behaviour, engagement and well-being. If we do not fulfil this essential motivator within us, we are unable to function fully. There are three important elements to achieving satisfaction in this area of motivation: autonomy, competence and relatedness.

What does this mean in a team context – is the individual team member able to satisfy their need to achieve a certain goal? Do they value the goal enough to put extra effort in for the pursuit of that goal? These psychological elements combine to deliver goal-directed behaviour, psychological development and well-being. All of this comes together to give potency to the goal, thus driving the individual to achieve it. The three psychological needs for this potent-driven outcome to evolve are: autonomy (is this a task that can be completed alone start to finish to contribute to the team or organizational aims?), competence (do individual team members possess the required knowledge and skills to achieve the goal?) and finally relatedness (does it mean something to that individual team member, does it have value for them to pursue the goal, does it mean something to the team?) Only if the individual is committed to the team and the team goal will the team become driven. These three needs are considered to be the foundation of the *what* and the *why* of the goal pursuit, i.e. they give fuel and reason to our effort to achieve a specific goal or outcome. For a goal to be achieved it requires an amount of personal striving. This striving will not occur if the goal is not related in some way to the individual or team.

Within a team, individuals will have specific roles and a unique contribution to make as part of the overall team process in achieving the team goal. If for any reason the individual does not feel the goal is worth pursuing, then it is less likely the team will achieve its joint outcome. Because self-determination theory operates at multiple levels, goal value, expectations and mechanisms to achieve a goal will collectively impact the effort to drive team members towards their goal.

It will be easier to establish joint goals and rally support behind goals where collaboration and trust exist, plus cohesion between team members. An appreciation of the complexity of setting appropriate and engaging goals for a team is a fine art, on the part of the manager or team leader, since the goal must appeal on both a personal and team level to be fully supported.

More information about self-determination theory and its links to self-motivation can be found here:

Deci, E.L. and Ryan, R.M. (1985). *Intrinsic Motivation and Self-Determination in Human Behavior*. New York: Plenum.

Effective team case study

If you have heard of Camp America and the concept of summer camps that are commonplace in the USA, you will know these activity retreats offer a summer-long adventure with the opportunity to learn new skills and make new friends. Certainly, a summer away from home, from family and one's familiar surroundings enables personal self-discovery and development. Filling the summer agenda calls for a variety of activities plus a particular event such as that of Colour Wars Week.

Colours Wars Week entails the whole population of the camp being split and affiliated with a red team or a blue team. For that week, each team member is expected to wear the team colour, with cabins across the camp also decorated in the team colour. A team song would be crafted and a team play presented on the finale of the Colour War Week. Everything the team members do during that week is for their team and is monitored, assessed and scored at every opportunity. Rivalry is hot and competition fierce. Some activities go on through the night, illustrating the commitment and connectedness to the team in an effort to gain better team scores and a better overall performance. Extra effort is expended around the clock. Every age, rank and role within the Camp, including staff and residents, is assigned to a team. Nothing else matters for the week.

This is possibly an example of teams and teaming unlike anything experienced in our workplace, but it reflects the essential elements of foundational team functioning we have been discussing.

Colour War Week takes place around two-thirds of the way through the summer camp of ten weeks, when the individual groups will have had time to get to know one another and hopefully bond. Campers will also have had time to share why they are there, what their personal goal is and what they hope to achieve. Everyone has a personal story to tell, often sharing stories around campfires toasting marshmallows, singing songs and getting to know one another better. Everyone shares a log cabin too – a good leveller, no matter what your personal circumstances or background. At Camp you are the same: a Camper, with a shared purpose to achieve your goal and return home a better person than at the start of the summer.

The particular camp experience in this case study is based on a weight loss Camp, specifically designed to support and assist campers to adopt a new and healthy regimen of eating and exercise. Each camper is weighed, measured and photographed (in their swimsuit) on arrival, resulting in a medically advised target weight aligned with their personal vision to be achieved by the end of the summer. All Campers relate to the shared value of being slimmer and healthier, not wanting to present themselves as they presently do, linking these feelings to a strong goal of their target weight. Every Camper shares this desire, with the support of their teammates to achieve their real individual goal. Being among others with similar values, experience and desire fuels the belief they can achieve their weight loss goals, in an environment of collective support and genuine desire to help and support one another.

Weekly weigh-ins and measurement of lost inches confirm the Campers' progress towards their target goals, inspiring and motivating fellow campers further. This is a time of celebration for what has been achieved and offers an opportunity to refocus on their ultimate goal – which now appears within reach. Progress may not be as radical for some, and in this instance colleagues, Campers and cabin buddies rally to support and lift the feelings of the Camper who may be disappointed with their apparent lack of progress.

In this case study, there are many similarities to that of building an effective supportive team. Once the target weight is achieved, the journey does not stop there; it is then about maintaining this performance in a manner similar to that of a team achieving peak performance and maintaining a high standard of excellence. Provided there is passion behind the goal setting, it can be maintained, aligned with individual values and the perceived outcome is worthy of the effort and individual trust. The process adopted during Camp to deliver the desired results can be adjusted to accommodate unique personal needs which can be tracked, through monitoring and measuring performance output, providing constant, relevant feedback.

Reflective questions

- To what extent is there a shared understanding of team purpose and values in my teams? If there is, what are the purpose and values? How do I know there is a shared understanding – what do I observe which tells me there is?
- When there is team challenge, does it support or challenge the purpose or values of the team? To what extent is there a possibility that it both supports and challenges the purpose and values? What might need to change to reconcile that?
- To what extent do my teams' purpose and values align with wider organizational purpose and values? What areas might be at odds or sit uncomfortably together?
- To what extent do I think my teams have shared goals? To what extent do I think my team members are able to translate my expectations of them with clarity?
- How are these organized into different members of my teams? Where and when are these coordinated? What are the vulnerabilities?
- Where in my teams would I say there is trust between team members? Where is trust weaker? What are the implications of this? To what extent does this offer challenge and to what extent is it useful for the functioning of my team?

References

Agrawal, V. (2012). Managing the diversified team: challenges and strategies for improving performance, *Team Performance Management: An International Journal*, 18(7/8): 384–400. http://dx.doi.org/10.1108/13527591211281129.

Amos, B. and Klimoski, R.J. (2014). Courage: making teamwork work well, *Group & Organization Management*, 39(1): 110–28. DOI: 10.1177/1059601113520407.

Buvik, M.P. and Tvedt, S.D. (2017). The influence of project commitment and team commitment on the relationship between trust and knowledge sharing in project teams, *Project Management Journal*, 48(2): 5.

Edmondson, A.C. (2012). Learning to team, *Leadership Excellence*, 29(8): 6.

Fleishman, E.A. (1992). Taxonomic efforts in the description of leader behavior: a synthesis and functional interpretation, *Leadership Quarterly*, 2(4): 245–87.

Ghosh, R., Shuck, B. and Petrosko, J. (2012). Emotional intelligence and organisational learning in work teams, *Journal of Management Development*, 31(6): 603–19.

Hackman, J.R. (2002). *Leading Teams: Setting the Stage for Great Performance*. Boston, MA: Harvard Business School Press.

Herzberg, F. (1966). *Work and the Nature of Man*. New York: World Publishing.

Herzberg, F., Mausner, B. and Snydermann, B. (1959). *The Motivation to Work*. New York: Wiley.

Katzenbach, J.R. and Smith, D.K. (1999). *The Wisdom of Teams: Creating the High-Performance Organization*. London: Harper Business.

Laud, R., Arevalo, J. and Johnson, M. (2016). The changing nature of managerial skills, mindsets and roles: advancing theory and relevancy for contemporary managers, *Journal of Management & Organization*, 22(4): 435–56.

Martin, L.J., Paradis, K.F., Eys, M.A. and Evans, B. (2013). Cohesion in sport: new directions for practitioners, *Journal of Sports Psychology in Action*, 4(1): 14–25.

Salas, E., Shuffler, M.L., Thayer, A.L., Bedwell, W.L., and Lazzara, E.H. (2015). Understanding and improving teamwork in organizations: a scientifically based practical guide, *Human Resource Management*, 54(4): 599–622. DOI:10.1002/hrm.21628.

Tuckman, B.W. (1965). Developmental sequence in small groups, *Psychological Bulletin*, 65(6): 384–99.

Psychology reference

Deci, E.L. and Ryan, R.M. (1985). *Intrinsic Motivation and Self-Determination in Human Behavior*. New York: Plenum.

4 Individual behaviour and its impact on the team

Summary

An appreciation of the behavioural impact of the team leader or manager on individual team members and that of team members on their colleagues is explored in this chapter, offering the rationale as to why, on occasions, activities do not go smoothly. Aside from exploring this impact on teams from a leader or manager's perspective, the chapter offers a clarification of the terms *management* and *leadership* by establishing clarity between the two fields of practice and their potential impacts on a team. According to Mintzberg's (1973) research, team managers reported that their responsibilities fell within three main areas: interpersonal, informational and decisional. In the interpersonal role of the manager, they act as a figurehead, a leader (through role modelling), and a liaison conduit from employees to senior management or external agencies (before the advent of flatter organizational structures). In the informational role managers monitor and disseminate information while acting as spokesperson on behalf of the team. In the final decisional role, managers can be expected to be disturbance handlers, resource allocators, negotiators and entrepreneurs. It is important to note that Mintzberg's classification of manager also includes elements of being a leader. As a simplistic differentiation, you may have heard the statement: *managers focus on tasks*, whereas *leaders focus on people*. Managers are in a position to ensure we do things right whereas a leader is in a position to ensure we do the right things. Managers direct, whereas leaders motivate. As there are subtle differences in terminology and interpretation in the manner with which managers and leaders conduct their activities, these can have an impact on the effectiveness of the team. Leading *what* and *how* is to be explored further in this book.

Keywords: managing and leading, behaviour and management practice of the team leader, team member perception of organizational support

Introduction

When we refer to the tasks of team leaders or managers, they would include the same issues of operational management, performance monitoring, target setting and talent management (Mintzberg 1973, 1990). Mintzberg's interviews with managers in the 1970s reassuringly illustrate that things have not changed, and reveal similar reports to the 30 managers interviewed for this book:

- The managerial activities carried out were often not logical, reasoned or orderly but tended to be broken up into discrete bursts of activity as demanded by individual team members, pending deadlines.
- Managers preferred to communicate verbally, spending an inordinate amount of time in meetings within their organizations or in meeting third parties externally, rather than dealing in written communication.

The distinction between leading and managing is often described simply as: leaders inspire actions, managers monitor actions. Leaders are also thought to innovate, develop, originate and challenge the status quo, whereas managers are expected to accept the status quo, administer, control and imitate to maintain standards (Sadun et al. 2017). In the flatter work structures discussed earlier, this may offer and drive the rationale for the traditional role differences of manager and leader to converge. Peter Drucker, regarded as somewhat of a guru, summarized management in five objectives (Bennis 2003):

1 setting objectives (or goals)
2 organizing
3 motivating and communicating
4 measuring performance
5 developing people

We can appreciate where the elements are placed when we traditionally think of leaders as setting the vision, inspiring followers, and as a consequence setting objectives. Drucker's list clearly resonates with the modern-day manager as not just being a list of the required activities of the team leader, but including and focusing on people and talent development.

Aims

Drucker's list is reliant on the manager's ability to interact with team members and the team in a constructive manner. This is generally held to be a vital social skill in the creation and maintenance of an effective team and organization (Drucker 1974/2011). There is a strong and varied literature base concerning teams and leadership, but significantly less linking the relationship between leader behaviour and team performance outcomes (Harvey et al. 2006 and Ewen et al. 2013, cited in Gerard et al. 2017). We will attempt to unpack some of the insights gained from the modern-day manager to create a deeper appreciation of the influential position team leaders have for teams.

Team leader or manager impact on team functioning

The role of the leader is vital in determining the outcome and adopted culture across all types of teams throughout an organization. There is clear recognition of the need to create conditions that inspire team members to unleash their self-potential and support one another (Herman 2014). Further, team leaders and managers need to set and create alignment between personnel and organizational goals, and between subgroups and team goals, developing strategic skills and helping team members articulate the values behind the organizational vision (Vincent-Hoper et al. 2012; Kunnanatt 2016). The setting and reviewing of appropriate, aligned goals is considered essential for creating forward traction which, as a consequence, includes the need for a level of mental cognition from team members. This understanding of the behaviour and standards needed to set the required goals and outcomes acts as a driver and an alignment force to facilitate the response of the team and its members. If the line manager or leader is unable to create these strong links and is uncertain of the objectives or required goals, they could be complicit in allowing a serious weakness within the team which hampers its ability to achieve and function fully.

In contrast with the role of the traditional manager, the team leader is a person more likely to facilitate employee learning and development by ensuring an understanding of the set goals, with a positive influence on team behaviour (Clutterbuck 2014). This is achieved through embedding feedback and reflection for the team members and the collective team. Thus, the manager and team leader would be delivering according to the findings of the Chartered Institute of Personnel and Development (CIPD 2015), which observed that the team manager or leader is best placed to address the developmental and learning needs of the team members. In this context, the manager or team leader is regarded as the lynchpin and therefore pivotal in ensuring the team achieves the desired organizational goals through alignment of team members and the creation of an effective working relationship. In so doing, the manager or team leader creates the positive belief and perception required of the organization for team members to align to. The behaviour of the manager or team leader is crucial for the success of the team, as will be explored further in the next section.

Behaviour and management practice of the team leader

For alignment, cohesion and mental closeness to be possible requires the team leader to highlight mutual appreciation of the contribution from each team member. This intra-team sharing is imperative for managers to positively engineer the appreciation and acceptance between team members. This aspect is based on the manager's awareness of the skills, unique experience and nuances that an individual member brings to the team, with skilled communication being essential for managers acting as engines of change (Ellinger et al. 2006).

Managers are in the key position to play the role of a communication intermediary by creating a positive leader–follower relationship that can impact the connection between leader *behaviour* and follower *reaction* and the evolution of a positive and supportive team environment. The quality of the leader–follower relationship defines the extent to which leadership behaviour influences employee performance, while negative attitudes cause employees to exhibit negative work behaviour (Hall 2013: 4). Translating the influence of the manager on creating a conducive working environment and its impact on the work environment is illustrated in Figure 4.1.

Figure 4.1 illustrates the reach and influence of the manager's behavioural impact and the contribution of this behaviour towards the evolution of a positive functioning team. Many commentators pinpoint manager behaviour as a pivotal element in its impact on team members from a positive and negative perspective. The CIPD also reports poor management and leadership practices as being the primary reason for employees resigning from an organization (CIPD 2017). These facts and statistics from the CIPD further support the importance of manager or leader behaviour for the performance of the team and the organization. As work life has become more dynamic and change is commonplace, there is an emphasis on the role of managerial behaviour in shaping employee performance and attitude (Kim et al. 2013; Peng and Lin 2016). Further research has expanded the importance of manager and team leader behaviour when reporting that the leadership style employed influences the emotional state of employees and subsequent job performance. The effectiveness of the manager and team leader is thus linked to their ability to manage their own feelings, moods and emotions as well as those of their team members (Agarwal et al. 2009). This links to the causation raised by Edmondson regarding team effectiveness that emotional intelligence increased stability and trust, improved learning and increased team outputs. The behaviour of managers and leaders does matter.

Figure 4.1 Influence of managers and team leaders

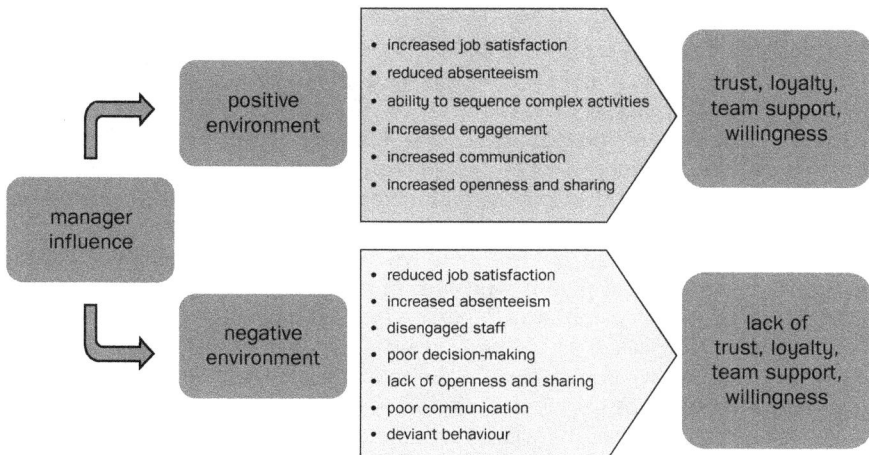

It has been postulated that employees with a poor manager or team leader–member relationship will likely reciprocate with comparable negative behaviour (Al-Nasser and Mohamed 2015). As mentioned earlier, adult learning is highly influenced by observation (Hur et al. 2011), with the behaviour displayed within teams setting expected standards (Peng and Lin 2016) and ultimately the team culture. The impact of the team (including that of the manager or team leader) does therefore have an influence on the behaviour of its members, which can affect learning and team performance. Managers and team leaders are to be cautioned in using the work team itself to influence and modify the attitudes, opinions and aspirations of the team members, even though they can learn positively from one another. Team learning through knowledge sharing is instrumental to the success of the team, but team individuals can also be negatively influenced by team members that possess a negative mindset.

The importance of mindset

Mindset is a belief concerning the nature of human behaviour and affects the opinion of the manager and team leader to the extent they can adjust, transform and develop the attitude or inclination of team members. If their mindset is not constructive or beneficial for the team it will impede peak performance. An open or closed mindset can support or inhibit the ability of the manager or team leader to facilitate positive change. When team members are open to sharing and understanding the skills and knowledge of their colleagues, patterns of behaviour evolve with a positive appreciation of key elements of shared tasks; this affects the anticipated needs and actions of the team and its ability to function (Rutti et al. 2012; Sun et al. 2017). It could be argued that creating this positive mental closeness or shared mindset becomes part of the team leader or manager's essential role in evolving a functional team. This shared psychological closeness or mindset results in a collective commitment, leading to a feeling of loyalty and desire to invest mentally and physically in the team achieving its organizational goals. This is a potential result if the manager or team leader can engineer and model this desired behaviour (Vincent-Hoper et al. 2012) and spotlights the importance of the manager or team leader's behaviour when observing that an attitude represents an evaluative disposition towards a certain situation, object or person (Santos and Passos 2013). This includes the perception that each team member may forge their opinion on the organizational employer, team member, line manager or team leader.

Building a positive team environment will not only have the above desirable outputs but also creates an improved working engagement with a line manager or team leader who is positioned to ensure the best possible outcome for each team member. The result is better sharing and openness of communication in terms of the knowledge gained by the manager or team leader of personal goals and ambitions for each team member, which facilitates the positive team engineering referred to earlier. This engineering and positive environment can bring about a desire *that going to work* is seen as enjoyable, thereby increasing job satisfaction. However, if communication channels between team members are not open, not transparent and not a healthy contributor towards a positive team environment, deviant behaviour can result. When combined with other outputs of a negative team environment such as increased absenteeism, disengagement and reduced job satisfaction, deviant behaviour is not conducive to a fully functional team and its delivery of joint organizational goals. Such deviance, once rooted, has other implications that will be addressed in Chapter.

When a manager or team leader has built a positive status with each team member it becomes an easier task to request that individuals carry out certain tasks and correctly sequence team activities. Conway and Coyle-Shapiro (2012) note that a worker who is proactively self-directed, flexible, versatile, driven by personal values and highly satisfied with their work will be less affected by uncertainty and more able to collaborate with other team members. The atmosphere surrounding such a team will offer a very positive perception of the manager, team leader and the organization, adding to a positive reputation inside and outside the organization. The perception stakeholders have of an organization impacts its success and ability to grow. As this perception is so important for the future reputation and growth of the organization, it will be explored further in the next section.

Team member perception of organizational support

Perception is important (Auer et al. 2014) as it represents the filter through which individuals evaluate information, appreciate roles and responsibilities, communicate, interact and execute, with a potential impact on interpersonal systems. Team context is influenced by the beliefs and feelings that each team member has about one another, and particularly mutual trust (Agarwal et al. 2009). Understanding how one is perceived by others in a team or in an organizational context is vitally important to leadership and managerial effectiveness (Otara 2011). Facilitative behaviour demonstrated by managers and leaders provides training (Ehrhardt et al. 2013) through observation of expected behaviours. Attitudes and actions adopted by managers and team leaders towards a team and its responsibilities can make a decisive difference in team member perception in the development of commitment (Bozer et al. 2013). Organizational actions that create visible differences among team members, such as bias or unfair treatment, have the potential to create less favourable attitudes towards line managers, team leaders and peers, resulting in increased turnover and decreased work-related assisting behaviour (Batson and Yoder 2012). When team members trust one another, they will have greater sensitivity to the needs of colleagues, more willingness to help and assist, and a greater likelihood of a positive social exchange (Bozer et al. 2013).

Perception of environmental characteristics such as management and leadership trust and support will affect the commitment of team members to the organization (Akron et al. 2016). Commitment is affected by perception in the form of internal and external compliance and internalization, and when aligned to a specific team purpose it could be viewed as supportive. For these commitment forms (internal and external, compliance and internalization) to improve with the resultant behaviour aimed at furthering the achievement of the team tasks is illustrative of a positive relationship. This is evidenced by an individual's propensity to trust others in the team and is based on the perceived trustworthiness of those team members. This leads to the behaviour of cooperation and collaboration, where less monitoring is required among team members in the knowledge that they are working with a trusted colleague. Increased trust through positive perception leads to a collaborative working status and easier management implications for the line manager or team leader.

As organizational roles have changed, a manager or team leader may need to place their interests aside for the collective well-being of the team members. This will assist in the achievement of organizational goals, with team members trusted to perform their tasks for the benefit of colleagues and the team. Expert observers comment that the hardest achievement for a manager is to improve people and cooperative corporate thinking simultaneously (Buvik and Tvedt 2017). A shared supportive style of leadership requires the coordinated distribution of knowledge and the integration of leadership skills among organizational members. This may be the only way to accommodate the fast-moving demands being made of teams. If team members do not witness or perceive evidence of commitment and support from managers or leaders, their commitment may wane. A contextual insight into the power of the team is that group dynamics can set the methods and procedures that enable individual personalities to influence opinion and team functioning. Other experts (e.g. Belschak and Den Hartok 2010; Buvik and Tvedt 2017) emphasize that it is not enough for managers or team leaders to consider the needs, goals or ideals of the team; they must address attitudes, motivations, opinions and aspirations to facilitate team cohesion and effective functioning. For high performance to be achieved, these issues were analysed further, with the suggestion that a higher order of team leadership and management is required, including an appreciation of the psychological needs of their members to make them feel valued and that their roles are worthwhile within the organization (Kanter 2010).

How these important messages are communicated is critical to the establishment of perceived perceptions. Companies and teams that build a culture of common respect through employee engagement, and influence the perception of incoming employees with a positive contagious spirit and work ethic, will reap performance rewards (a positive contagion). When their perceived impact on the team is considered, leaders and managers cannot afford to display a shallow level of engagement. To generate the desired commitment and performance from team members and be *perceived* with belief (Zoltan 2015) and authenticity requires the appropriate level of leadership and management behaviour to be an integral part of organizational strategy and goals.

Research strongly suggests that factors such as fairness can create a positive reward or a negative threatening consequence which influences an individual's perception of work-related attitudes and behaviour (Wells and Peachey 2010). Team leader and managerial behaviour that reinforces the desired organizational behaviour can actively encourage collective striving, enabling a team to weather demanding conditions more readily (Shahid and Shahid 2013). While team diversity is not easily detectable, team behaviour as the sum of the individual contributions from team members is (Kim et al. 2013). Diversity is determined by how team members perceive it (Schoenung and Dikova 2016) within the organization and their team. As a minority member, would an employee perceive the organization or their team as being inclusive? Would they be accepted? Would there be any undercurrents from a colleague to make them feel uncomfortable or not worthy to be part of this team? If the response is affirmative, the potential of the team to function fully will be impaired, possibly even before the team is brought together.

The manager or team leader's understanding of the impact of multiple pressures on employee behaviour and attitude has important implications (Akron et al. 2016) for enticing and retaining skilled employees, as well as for being perceived as a fair, progressive, supportive employer. The role of the team leader or manager in this transference is critical. Organizational culture can further impact employee behaviour due to it being the conduit for the vision and values of its leaders, reward schemes, stories and shared experiences. If the perception received from these stories and messages does not align with the values or career aspirations of the individual, the organization can be damaged. This has a consequence for the ability to hire the necessary skills, to flourish and grow as intended as an organization. As the face of the organization, it is the responsibility of the line manager or team leader to forge a team culture that entices and maintains an appeal for recruits and existing team members. Where the narrative of the organizational culture displays distrust, indifference, lack of involvement and resistance to change, the perception of the organization would not be positive, resulting in a diminished capacity from employees. Observers such as Yang (2015) argue that behaviour is influenced by the environment, which is supported when revealing that negative feelings inhibit social integration. Where the environment is uncertain or adverse, negative emotions will result (Staddon 2010, cited in Nansubuga et al. 2015). This observation is reinforced when noting that team members share emotions as well as cognition. If negative, the situation can induce stress and deplete positive mental capacity (Yang et al. 2015). Thus, perception is important from a line manager or team leader perspective as well as for their team (Dimas et al. 2016).

Psychological underpinning

You may be familiar with the statement that 'no one goes to work to do a bad job'. This statement offers a useful platform and foundation for the psychological approach that truly believes this to be the case, that each team member is at work to do their best, and as a line manager or team leader if we develop a strong trusting relationship we can bring out the very best each team member can offer via a *person-centred approach*.

The foundation of this school of thought is based on the findings and teachings of the psychologist Carl Rogers (1959, 1961). A person-centred approach can be applied to individuals (solo or as team members) for health improvement, educational progress and conflict resolution. We will revisit this application in conflict resolution later in this book.

Carl Rogers used the person-centred approach to facilitate or as a means of achieving self-determination – having discussed this in the last chapter we know the importance and value in developing self-determination. In simplistic terms a person-centred approach applied by a line manager or team leader is a means of developing and fostering the desired internal self-determination, drive and motivation in each employee, aligned with their personal and team goals. It is a managerial or team leader stance, that if consistently and authentically applied will build a strong, trusting relationship with each team member.

Carl Rogers proposed that human beings have the propensity towards growth, development and optimal functioning, described as a self-actualizing tendency which is part of self-determination. But these tendencies benefit from the support of an aligning manager or team leader, who believes in you and your skills as an individual and who is able to create the correct social environment for each employee to feel aligned and accepted to then flourish. This correct social environment Rogers posited is one where the individual feels understood, valued and accepted for the experience and skills they bring to the team, not just by the manager or team leader but also other team members. It is this correct team social environment that the manager or team leader must evolve and protect for every team member to function fully.

Rogers suggested there were six stages to achieving this social state of congruence and alignment:

1 two people in psychological alignment – understanding and appreciation between employee and manager or team leader and vice versa
2 the employee being in a state of incongruence – as when a new employee joins a team the manager/team leader facilitates alignment
3 line manager is congruent with organizational goals and vision – and as manager or team leader committed to facilitating alignment of each team member
4 manager or team leader has unconditional positive regard for the employee – fostering mutual respect
5 manager or team leader is emotionally intelligent and appreciates individual employees – manager or team leader appreciates each employee and communicates with them for mutual gain and goal achievement in a social environment
6 communication and empathy achieved – manager or team leader encourages empathy between team members

These are the stages to facilitate the constructive expression of the actualizing tendency referred to earlier, enabling the way towards positive constructive relationships.

Case study

Throughout the recent Covid pandemic, we have witnessed how various organizations have dealt with the challenging needs of the marketplace and those of their employees. From one end of this accommodating spectrum to the other, there have been examples of companies firing employees without notice or severance pay, to companies allowing their staff to work from home with a phased return to an office environment as the impact of the pandemic has lessened. Many companies will have also offered well-being programmes and support for those bereaved, with the flexibility to accommodate child tutoring or care.

News broadcasts and social media pronouncements concerning the behaviour of these organizations will have had an impact on their standing. The perception of their employees along with the public will have been changed according to how their organizations have dealt with the challenging environment.

The perception of these organizations will now be embedded in our collective memory as to whether they were viewed as good or not so good employers. The impact is far-reaching, as witnessed by the airlines and airports trying to recruit staff they have 'let go' during the pandemic, now unable to replace those employees. Many employees have been reluctant to rejoin their previous employer, with many finding alternative employment with organizations that they perceive value them more. Similar cases have been reported for service sector workers, restaurants, cafes and retail outlets, with many establishments not surviving the impact of the pandemic at all.

Which organizations have you changed your perception of and why? What can we learn from this experience – will that alter how we create the right perception in our team?

Reflective questions

- What is my role in setting my teams' objectives or goals? To what extent does that support or remove the teams' ability to set their own goals?
- How might that be impacting their motivation or ability to meet their goals or their well-being? What are alternatives to the current approach, and how might that influence any present team challenge?
- What is my role in organizing the configuration of my teams and how they organize themselves? To what extent does that support or remove the teams' ability to organize themselves?
- How might that be impacting their motivation or ability to meet their goals or their well-being? What are alternatives to the current approach, and how might that influence any present team challenge?
- What is my role in motivating the teams? What am I observing which suggests this approach is working, or not?

- What is my approach to measuring team performance? To what extent does the approach influence individual behaviour, and team behaviour, in terms of how the team is rewarded or penalized?
- What do I observe which might suggest that this approach could be a source of challenge?
- What is my role in developing people?
- To what extent do my teams decide their individual or collective development as a team?
- To what extent do the individuals in my teams support each other as a way to support team development?
- What organizational support do my teams most value?
- What approach is there across the organization to support managers, leaders and team leaders?
- To what extent am I known as being empathetic as a leader? What about other leaders, managers or team leaders? To what extent do I feel I have a positive, constructive relationship with my team members?
- What areas do I think are missing to enable a positive, constructive relationship (what, and with whom, specifically)?

References

Agarwal, R., Angst, C.M. and Magni, M. (2009). The performance effects of coaching: a multilevel analysis using hierarchical linear modelling, *International Journal of Human Resource Management*, 20(10): 2110–34. DOI: 10.1080/09585190903178054.

Akron, S., Feinblit, O., Hareli, S. and Tzafrir, S.S. (2016). Employment arrangements diversity and work group performance, *Team Performance Management*, 22(5/6): 310–30. http://dx.doi.org/10.1108/TPM-11-2015-0053.

Al-Nasser, A. and Mohamed, B. (2015). Examining the relationship between organizational coaching and workplace counterproductive behaviours in the United Arab Emirates, *International Journal of Organizational Analysis*, 23(3): 378–403. DOI: 10.1108/IJOA-08-2014-0793.

Auer, J.C., Kao, C.-Y., Hemphill, L., Johnston, E.W. and Teasley, S.D. (2014). The uncertainty challenge of contingent collaboration, *Human Resource Management Journal*, 24(4): 531–47.

Batson, V.D. and Yoder, L.H. (2012). Managerial coaching: a concept analysis, *Journal of Advanced Nursing*, 68(7.6): 1658–69. doi: 10.1111/j.1365-2648.2011.05840.x.

Belschak, F.D. and Den Hartog, D.N. (2010). Pro-self, pro-social, and pro-organizational foci of proactive behaviour: differential antecedents and consequences, *Journal of Occupational and Organizational Psychology*, 83(2): 475–98.

Bennis, W. (2003). *On Becoming a Leader: The Leadership Classic*. Oxford: Perseus.

Bozer, G., Sarros, J.C. and Santora, J. C. (2013). The role of coachee characteristics in executive coaching for effective sustainability, *Journal of Management Development*, 32(3): 277–94. DOI: 10.1108/02621711311318319.

Buvik, M.P. and Tvedt, S.D. (2017). The influence of project commitment and team commitment on the relationship between trust and knowledge sharing in project teams, *Project Management Journal*, 48(2): 5.

CIPD (Chartered Institute of Personnel and Development) (2015). *Getting Under the Skin of Workplace Conflict: Tracing the Experiences of Employees.* London: CIPD. Available at: https://www.cipd.co.uk/Images/getting-under-skin-workplace-conflict_2015-tracing-experiences-employees_tcm18-10800.pdf (accessed 13 January 2023).

CIPD (Chartered Institute of Personnel and Development) (2017). *Employee Outlook: Employee Views on Working Life.* London: CIPD.

Clutterbuck, D. (2014). Team coaching, in E. Cox, T. Bachkirova and D. Clutterbuck (eds), *The Complete Handbook of Coaching,* 2nd edn. London: Sage Publications, pp. 271–84.

Conway, N. and Coyle-Shapiro, J.A.M. (2012). The reciprocal relationship between psychological contract fulfilment and employee performance and the moderating role of perceived organisational support and tenure, *Journal of Occupational and Organizational Psychology,* 85(2): 277–99.

Dimas, I.D., Lourenço, P.R. and Rebelo, T. (2016). The effects on team emotions and team effectiveness of coaching in interprofessional health and social care teams, *Journal of Interprofessional Care,* 30(4): 416–22. DOI: 10.3109/13561820.2016.1149454.

Drucker, P.F. (1974/2011). *Management: an abridged and revised version of Management: Tasks, Responsibilities, Practices.* London: Routledge.

Ehrhardt, K., Miller, J.S., Freeman, S.J. and Hom, P.W. (2013). Examining project commitment in cross-functional teams: antecedents and relationship with team performance, *Journal of Business and Psychology,* 29(3): 443–61. DOI: 10.1007/s10869-013-9325.

Ellinger, A.D., Beattie, R.S., Hamlin, R.G., Wang, Y. and Trolan, O. (2006). The manager as coach: a review of empirical literature and the development of a tentative model of managerial coaching, in F. Poell (ed.) *Proceedings of the Seventh International Conference on HRD Research and Practice across Europe.* Tilburg: University of Tilburg.

Gerard, L., McMillan, J. and D'Annunzio-Green, N. (2017). Conceptualising sustainable leadership, *Industrial and Commercial Training,* 49(3): 116–26.

Hall, J.L. (2013). Managing teams with diverse compositions: implications for managers from research on the faultline model, *Advanced Management Journal,* 78(1): 4–10.

Herman, H.M.Tse (2014). Linking leader–member exchange differentiation to work team performance, *Leadership & Organization Development Journal,* 35(8): 710–24.

Hur, Y., van den Berg, P.T. and Wilderon, C.P.M. (2011). Transformational leadership as a mediator between emotional intelligence and team outcomes, *Leadership Quarterly,* 22(4): 591–603.

Kanter, R.M. (2010). *Supercorp: How Vanguard Companies Create Innovation, Profits, Growth, and Social Good.* London: Profile Books.

Kim, S., E, T.M., Kim, W. and Kim, J. (2013). The impact of managerial coaching behavior on employee work-related reactions, *Journal of Business and Psychology,* 28(3): 315–30.

Kunnanatt, J.T. (2016). 3D leadership – strategy-linked leadership framework for managing teams, *Economics, Management, and Financial Markets,* 11(3): 30–55.

Mintzberg, H. (1973). *The Nature of Managerial Work.* New York: Harper & Row.

Mintzberg, H. (1990). The manager's job: folklore and fact, *Harvard Business Review,* 68(2): 163–76.

Nansubuga, F., Munene, J.C. and Ntayi, J.M. (2015). Can reflection boost competences development in organisations?, *European Journal of Training and Development,* 39(6): 504–21. http://dx.doi.org/10.1108/EJTD-01-2015-0004.

Otara, A. (2011). Perception: a guide for managers and leaders, *Journal of Management and Strategy,* 2(3): 21–4.

Peng, J.C. and Lin, J. (2016). Linking supervisor feedback environment to contextual performances: the mediating effect of leader–member exchange, *Leadership & Organization Development Journal,* 37(6): 802–20.

Rutti, R.M., Ramsey, J.R. and Chenwei, L. (2012). The role of other orientation in team selection and anticipated performance, *Team Performance Management: An International Journal*, 18(1/2): 41–58.

Sadun, R., Bloom, N. and Van Reenen, J. (2017). Why do we undervalue competent management, *Harvard Business Review*, Sept–Oct.

Santos, C.M. and Passos, A.M. (2013). Team mental models, relationship conflict and effectiveness over time, *Team Performance Management*, 19(7/8): 363–85.

Schoenung, B. and Dikova, D. (2016). Reflections on organizational team diversity research in search of a logical support to an assumption, *Equality, Diversity and Inclusion: An International Journal*, 35(3): 221–31.

Shahid, A. and Shahid, M. (2013). Gaining employee commitment: linking to organisational effectiveness, *Journal of Management Research*, 5(1): 250.

Sun, H., Pei-Lee, T. and Karis, H. (2017). Team diversity, learning, and innovation: a mediation model, *Journal of Computer Information Systems*, 57(1): 22–30.

Vincent-Hoper, S., Muser, C. and Janneck, M. (2012). Transformational leadership, work engagement and occupational success, *Career Development International*, 17(7): 663–82.

Wells, J. and Peachey, J.W. (2010). Turnover intentions: do leadership behaviors and satisfaction with the leader matter?, *Team Performance Management: An International Journal*, 17(1/2): 23–40.

Yang, I. (2015). The positive outcomes of 'Socially Sharing Negative Emotions' in work teams: a conceptual exploration, *European Management Journal*, 34(2): 172–81.

Yang, M.-Y., Cheng, F.-C. and Chuang, A. (2015). The role of affects in conflict frames and conflict management, *International Journal of Conflict Management*, 26(4): 427–49.

Zoltan, R. (2015). Group dynamics and team functioning in an organisational context, *Ecoforum*, 4(2): 154–8.

Psychology references

Rogers, C.R. (1959). A theory of therapy, personality and interpersonal relationships as developed in the client-centered framework, cited in Greene, R.R. (ed.) (2017). *Human Behavior Theory & Social Work Practice*. Abingdon and New York: Routledge, p. 45.

Rogers, C.R. (1961). *On Becoming a Person: A Therapist's View of Psychotherapy*. London: Constable.

5 Understanding dysfunctional behaviour

Summary

This chapter explores team challenge attributed to dysfunctional behaviour as experienced by the interviewed team leaders and managers employing a coaching style with their teams. We explore the potential origins of dysfunctional behaviour and its impact within the team. Understanding the origins of dysfunctional behaviour is a critical platform for prevention of such behaviour and to enable a foundation for positive change in teams. This is an essential chapter for any manager or leader to reflect upon critically if they wish to engineer a healthy, fully functioning team. Setting the team foundation in place will reap multiple benefits for each team member, including those leading and managing the team, through establishing a platform for peak performance.

Keywords: dysfunctional behaviour, organizational culture creating dysfunction, manager influence

Introduction

In the most simplistic of descriptions, dysfunctional behaviour falls within the broad category of antisocial behaviour, which is described as behaviour that brings about harm or is intended to bring harm to an organization, its employees or stakeholders (Giacalone and Greenberg 1997, cited in Van Fleet and Griffin 2015). Dysfunctional behaviour may range from antisocial behaviour such as inappropriateness (behaviour and language) to sabotaging a project or aggressive behaviour towards a team member or against the organization itself. Two experts who have researched the area of dysfunctional behaviour have evolved a list referred to as the Dysfunctional Dozen (Jurkiewicz and Giacalone 2016): deception, dependency, distrust, egoism, immediacy, impiety, impunity, inequality, inhumanity, invariance, narcissism and obduracy. Personal dysfunctional behaviour can result in great potential challenge for any manager or team leader, as defined by workplace deviance, theft, dishonesty and aggression (Van Fleet and Griffin 2015).

Aims

This chapter aims to assist managers and team leaders in recognizing the importance of dysfunctional behaviour, and explores inter alia the Dysfunctional Dozen to alert managers and leaders to the behaviours that need to be recognized and apprehended for the good of the team.

Understanding dysfunctional behaviour

Managers describe their team as challenging when the following behaviours are observed: underperformance, time wasting, developing unproductive patterns (Maruping et al. 2015) such as hoarding work and not being willing to delegate (Ehrhardt et al. 2013), poor communication (Egan and Hamlin 2014), lacking trust (Boies et al. 2015), lack of flexibility, lacking follow-up (not taking responsibility), not being proactive (Belschak and Den Hartog 2010) or taking ownership of tasks (Karaçivi and Demirel 2014). The presence of any of these behavioural traits can impede the function of any team member.

One specific challenge for managers and team leaders is when disagreements or interpersonal conflicts are allowed to manifest. These can spiral rapidly into a dysfunctional working relationship with the potential to impede collaboration and cohesion (Driskell et al. 2017). Kaufmann (2012) makes the link that challenging behaviour can evolve into dysfunctional behaviour if it is allowed to occur or remains unchecked by the manager or team leader. Dysfunctional behaviour manifests as personal quarrelling, ineffective decision-making and suboptimal performance. A dysfunctional working relationship is unproductive, which in the long term can prevent individuals and teams reaching their full effective performance (Santos and Passos 2013). These issues have the capability of holding the team back from achieving peak potential. Conflict avoidance is a major contributor to dysfunctional relationships within a team due to poor communication (Santos and Passos 2013) or where intimidation arises from uncomfortable issues that need to be raised openly for discussion. Experts on team functioning (Gerard et al. 2017) reiterate that effective, open communication is the necessary conduit between individual actions and organizational purpose. The purpose of the line manager or team leader is to align this dialogue. Line managers and team leaders are further encouraged to connect with the *receptors of meaning* (Fairhurst and Connaughton 2014), thereby providing individual drivers for each team member to collectively function in a seamless capacity. Creating a positive mental closeness (Zoltan 2015) links the individual to the task by fostering a close understanding between team members and the organization.

There is potential for individuals (unintentionally or otherwise) to possess a predisposition towards dysfunctional behaviour under circumstances arising from differences in genetic and biological factors, values, personality traits, experiences and motives. To counter this possibility, one instruction from Zoltan (2015), a team expert, is for line managers and team leaders to *know* the team member's attributes by *knowing* their background, their personality, their values and experience. This can result from an interview process or team bonding activities.

Further, *knowing* the specific characteristics of a team member is critical to discerning when the individual may be distracted or not quite behaving in their normal manner. This offers an opportunity for the manager or team leader to intervene as necessary. Individual characteristics can have a detrimental effect on team performance due to their predilection towards interpersonal and relational conflict arising from distortions in social information processing (Boies et al. 2015; Yang et al. 2015): if an individual is distracted, worried or concerned over an issue, they can have difficulty in focusing and taking on additional information to that already weighing on their thoughts. The ability of a line manager or team leader to recognize this state in any of their employees will facilitate an ideal opportunity to provide personal support, thereby preventing escalation and a negative result in a wider team context.

Line managers, team leaders and employees must understand their mutual limitations to avoid unproductive behaviours as related to the standard setting and observational examples mentioned earlier (Al-Nasser and Mohamed 2015). The team and its organizational environment or culture can initiate personal dysfunctional behaviour via pressures, stress, presence of negative and untrusting attitudes, unclear performance goals or lack of appropriate feedback, perceived unfair treatment (of self or a colleague) and violations of trust. These conditions can arise when there is a deviation from expected standards. All these issues have been identified as organizational factors with the potential to promote deviant behaviour (Van Fleet and Griffin 2015). Other listed non-productive behaviours are victimization, hostility, verbal, mental or physically inappropriate behaviour, undermining, harassment, aggression, unwelcome and unfriendly confrontation, social isolation, the silent treatment, excessive criticism or monitoring, discrepancies, gossiping, being assigned unreasonable workloads, deadlines or tasks, indifference, depriving of responsibility, withholding information and lack of candid feedback (Al-Nasser and Mohamed 2015).

In summary, any of the above behavioural traits arising from just one team member can impact the culture of the whole team, impeding individual performance and the ability to function as a cohesive, collaborative team. This would not make the guilty team member popular with their colleagues and is likely to perpetuate a declining spiral. It is important to highlight that organizations per se can be dysfunctional, resulting in dysfunctional individuals (Jurkiewicz and Giacalone 2016) and therefore teams. This is particularly apt if a large percentage of our lives is spent at work, whether working as part of a team or individually. When an employee is interviewed or hired from another organization, this may be an important consideration: has the individual been influenced by a previous (dysfunctional) culture, and if so, do they have a propensity for change?

Organizational culture creating dysfunction

Organizational culture can impact employee behaviour since it is the conduit for the vision and values of its managers and leaders, reward schemes, stories, shared experience and standards. Research reaffirms that hierarchies in organizations can foster dysfunctional behaviour that prevents the achievement of organizational goals by inhibiting clear communication (Jurkiewicz and Giacalone 2016) and interdepartmental cooperation. The recognition of the negative impact of hierarchical structures may be a positive driver towards delayering in favour of flatter structures as is commonplace in some modern organizations. The intention of such a measure would be to improve communication flow and the speed of decision-making, which further adds to the expectations placed on the line manager or team leader.

The interaction of organizational culture with individuals can work in a positive or negative manner. Negatively perceived consequences can influence employee work-related behaviour and attitudes (Al-Nasser and Mohamed 2015) if employees perceive, for example, a reward scheme being withdrawn, threatened or changed. Furthermore, negativity can create a propensity to elicit dysfunctional behaviour (Van Fleet and Griffin 2015). Line managers and team leaders need to be cognizant that an organizational culture displaying distrust, indifference, lack of involvement and resistance to change (Al-Nasser and Mohamed 2015) will likely create a diminished capacity from employees. If we recall, teams are social constructs (Dimas et al. 2016) and processing of social information suggests that individual behaviour within teams is likely guided by behavioural displays from others in that environment. It is an important task of managerial and team leaders to therefore ensure team behaviour is healthy, which reaffirms that behaviour is heavily influenced by the environment (Yang 2015). Further research (Staddon 2010, cited in Nansubuga et al. 2015; Van Fleet and Griffin 2015) supports this narrative, revealing that negative feelings inhibit social integration while negative emotions result from an uncertain or adverse environment. This supports the observation that team members share emotions as well as cognition, which if negative can induce stress and deplete mental capacity (Dimas et al. 2016).

Social integration is the umbrella construct (Mahlendorf 2015) that managers and team leaders must engineer to prevent the rise of dysfunctional behaviour in teams. Dysfunctional teams and organizations generally fail to achieve their goals and are frequently slated for poor management and leadership. To avoid dysfunctional consequences, focus is generally directed towards increasing line manager and team leader accountability (Zoltan 2015) or advocating that managers and team leaders pay attention to individual characteristics such as desires, needs, goals, ideals and motives (Smith and Brummel 2013). Happy individuals make happy teams.

Other researchers suggest that a dysfunctional organizational culture becomes apparent when the leaders or managers possess poor people skills (Gerard et al. 2017). This reinforces the advice offered to line managers and team leaders to create a dynamic connection with their team members

(Aquila 2007). One reported observation is that the biggest hurdle for managers and team leaders is not just the problem of identifying underperformance, but an inability to deal with challenge – an issue the manager or team leader should not tackle alone. Another perspective encourages line managers and team leaders to exhibit caution when using the team itself as a means of creating positive action (Zoltan 2015). The notion that team activity can improve interpersonal relationships and social integration by sharing and dispelling negative emotions in team members is a useful ploy as a management tactic (Yang et al. 2015). Away days and team-building activities have a role to play here, if well administered.

Influence of manager and team leader

Managers and team leaders need to be capable of engaging the team to facilitate the alignment of each team member. The ability of the manager or team leader to recognize and identify potentially disruptive characteristics is a critical and preventative step to avoid derailing and inducing dysfunctional behaviour within a team. To elaborate, Table 5.1 illustrates the expert findings from Keyton (1999), Aquila (2007: 14), Kaufmann (2012) and Kiefer and Barclay (2012) relating unproductive or dysfunctional behaviour with the collective behavioural aspects from each author, collated into summary behaviours.

This table offers a critical checklist for line managers and team leaders to analyse potential dysfunctional behaviours in their team members. As a line manager or team leader, there is a need to alert those in the team who are on the periphery and do not engage fully or participate in team events. This type of isolation does not foster bonding, trust or a wide appreciation of individual team member skills and their contribution to the team. Mental closeness would never evolve in such a context. The team member who often misunderstands or misconstrues instructions or tasks can create confusion within the team; which similarly applies to a specific team member who is always at the centre of any disturbance. The line manager or team leader needs to be aware if there is a team member saying or doing the wrong things, upsetting other colleagues – possibly due to a lack of emotional intelligence or worse, a personality disorder leading to emotional outbursts through unregulated emotions, leading to a situation where no team member knows the best method of approach on any given day due to uncertainty as to which emotion will be reciprocated. The line manager or team leader cannot ignore any difficult situations that may arise from an individual becoming toxic for the whole team. Are team tasks missing delivery timelines or quality standards? Does this always involve the same individuals? Such scenarios should lead line managers and team leaders to delve deeper into identifying the cause. The solution may be as simple as a training requirement or something more specific relating to the checklist in Table 5.1.

Table 5.1 Comparative descriptors of unproductive or dysfunctional behaviour

Keyton 1999	Aquila 2007	Kaufmann 2012	Kiefer and Barclay 2012	Summary behaviours
interactions create confusion	do not communicate well	prevent team being	effective	poor communication
problematic	manipulative	prone to disagreements	emotions – unregulated	emotional imbalance
confuse situations	hoard work – unwilling to delegate	ineffective decision-making	reduce energy	inhibiting team flow
want to be centre of attention	not a team player	abnormal or impaired behaviour	create attentional demands	not a team player
negative attitude	do not participate in team events	prone to quarrelling	show negative emotions	negative attitude
primary provoker in disruption	things can only be done their way	difference of opinion	disconnected not engaged	provoker of disruption
deviant behaviour	become overly aggressive	passive aggressive	diminished psychological health	deviant behaviour
seek a scapegoat – never them	never their fault	absence of shared responsibility	attention away from task	do not take responsibility
displace others	let the team down	increased implementation problems	toxic to whole team	toxic to team
increase stress for whole team	unable to deliver	sub-optimal performer	draining for whole team	sub-optimal behaviour

Table 5.1 (*Continued*)

Keyton 1999	Aquila 2007	Kaufmann 2012	Kiefer and Barclay 2012	Summary behaviours
unable to sustain role in isolation	drive staff away, isolated	ineffective		**isolationist**
trigger discord	let the team down	dissent		**discordant**
plant doubts	do not trust colleagues	non trusting		**undermine trust**
	lack emotional intelligence	frustrating		**not emotionally intelligent**
	unrealistic promises	lacklustre decision-making		**poor decision-making**
	work too few hours to produce desired output	polar opposite of functional		**non functional**
	false threats	conflict allowed to spiral		**threatening**
	fail to follow up	increased risk		**disengagement**
	often accept wrong type of work	increased operational issues		**not functional**
	insecure			**insecurity**

It is imperative therefore that the behavioural characteristics of individual team members are viewed as pivotal to the functioning of the team and the attainment of organizational goals. Senge (1990) makes a valuable point that we cannot necessarily create a *new* team culture, but as a line manager or team leader we can create an environment within which a *positive* cohesive culture can evolve with a platform for the new team culture to flourish. For a team to be a success, the line manager or team leader needs to create an environmental climate for a functioning team to evolve through effective management and leadership.

We shall start to analyse how this can be done in Chapter 6.

Psychological underpinning

Positive psychology focuses on how to get the best out of an individual or team, and may be an appropriate lens through which to describe what needs to be applied to help bring change in a dysfunctional team situation. Understanding psychology and how the human brain works has developed apace in recent decades, allowing us to appreciate tried and tested practice on a different level – even from a practice perspective we knew worked but didn't quite understand how or why. Some of these unknowns are being revealed with improved technology to assist our understanding of the brain and its physical and mental attributes.

Positive psychology is focused on maximizing an individual's functioning. Originally identified by Martin Seligman in 1998, building on numerous foundational forefathers such as Carl Rogers (see Chapter 4) and Maslow (of Hierarchy of Needs acclaim) while directing attention to attaining well-being vs. *fixing* a person who may not be fully functioning. In this sense, this branch of psychology focuses on positive outcomes, positive behaviour and the positive contribution that an individual can make to the team. The subliminal drip-feeding of positive focus also has an impact on team members – the positive contagion, energizing them into positive action, possibly even when they don't feel like it.

Positive psychology is focused on what the individual's strengths and capabilities are, and builds on these as a foundation for forward positive progression. This can enhance and improve performance, at the same time offering a reference point for the individual to perform something they can already do with a small stretch element. This can give an individual that extra confidence required.

Seligman published updates in 2011 on his original work, with the introduction of his PERMA model – Positive emotions, Engagement, Relationships, Meaning and Achievement. Each of these elements lend themselves perfectly to the development of a fully functional team, by checking whether each team member is in a positive emotional state and able to contribute positively to the team activities (be engaged), forge productive relationships with the line manager or team leader and team members, and create meaning and achieve the tasks in hand. In addition to PERMA offering a check-in framework, this will further provide an opportunity to align the self-determination as discussed previously to enhance positive mental closeness among the team members. Through using PERMA based on the individual strengths of each team member as the platform for a line manager or team leader, a team member discussion builds the connectedness and trust required of the individual and the contribution they can make, thereby enhancing the *feeling of belonging* in the team.

Positive psychology offers an easy to apply and potentially powerful framework for supporting team functioning.

Reflective questions

- What have I observed about my organization's culture which may be creating dysfunctional behaviour? What ways of working or interacting with each other might be a source of dysfunctional behaviour? Who else might be observing the same, or different? What does this tell me about what I might do to intervene and who can help the change?
- To what extent are the dysfunctional behaviours I am observing permanent (displayed all the time) or situational (in certain contexts)? If the latter, in what circumstances might those behaviours arise, e.g. where, what, when and with whom? What might this tell me about how to diagnose the situation and my next step?
- Where might behaviours indicate to me that there could be developmental needs? What specific skills might be needed in those cases? Might there be purpose or value level differences which could be more difficult to develop? When and where might coaching be offered?
- To what extent do I or others promote positive emotions, engagement, relationships, meaning or achievement? For each, what do I observe working or not? What does that tell me about what I can try next, when I next see dysfunctional behaviour?
- To what extent is dysfunctional behaviour widespread in my organization? What might be the wider cause of this? How well known is this knowledge? How is working in this context affecting me and my teams, and how might I respond with my/their longer-term health in mind?

References

Al-Nasser, A. and Mohamed, B. (2015). Examining the relationship between organizational coaching and workplace counterproductive behaviours in the United Arab Emirates, *International Journal of Organizational Analysis*, 23(3): 378–403. DOI: 10.1108/IJOA-08-2014-0793.

Aquila, A.J. (2007). Dealing with underperforming or dysfunctional partners, *CPA Practice Management Forum* [online], June 3(6).

Belschak, F.D. and Den Hartog, D.N. (2010). Pro-self, pro-social, and pro-organizational foci of proactive behaviour: differential antecedents and consequences, *Journal of Occupational and Organizational Psychology*, 83(2): 475–98.

Boies, K., Fiset, J. and Gill, H. (2015). Communication and trust are key: unlocking the relationship between leadership and team performance and creativity, *Leadership Quarterly*, 26: 1080–94. http://dx.doi.org/10.1016/j.leaqua.

Dimas, I.D., Lourenço, P.R. and Rebelo, T. (2016). The effects on team emotions and team effectiveness of coaching in interprofessional health and social care teams, *Journal of Interprofessional Care*, 30(4): 416–22. DOI: 10.3109/13561820.2016.1149454.

Driskell, T., Salas, E. and Driskell, J.E. (2017). Teams in extreme environments: alterations in team development and teamwork, *Human Resource Management Review*, 28(4): 434–49. http://dx.doi.org/10.1016/j.hrmr.2017.01.002.

Egan, T. and Hamlin, R.G. (2014). Coaching, HRD, and relational richness: putting the pieces together, *Advances in Developing Human Resources*, 16(2): 242–57.

Ehrhardt, K., Miller, J.S., Freeman, S.J. and Hom, P.W. (2013). Examining project commitment in cross-functional teams: antecedents and relationship with team performance, *Journal of Business and Psychology*, 29(3): 443–61. DOI: 10.1007/s10869-013-9325.

Fairhurst, G. and Connaughton, S.L. (2014). Leadership: a communication perspective, *Leadership*, 10(1): 7–35. DOI: 10.1177/1742715013509396.

Gerard, L., McMillan, J. and D'Annunzio-Green, N. (2017). Conceptualising sustainable leadership, *Industrial and Commercial Training*, 49(3): 116–26.

Jurkiewicz, C.L. and Giacalone, R.A. (2016). Organizational determinants of ethical dysfunctionality, *Journal of Business Ethics*, 136(1): 1–12. DOI: 10.1007/s10551-014-2344-z.

Karaçivi, A. and Demirel, A. (2014). A futuristic commentary: coach-like leadership, *International Journal of Business and Social Science*, 5(9): 126–33.

Kaufmann, B. (2012). The anatomy of dysfunctional working relationships, *Business Strategy Series*, 13(2): 102–6.

Keyton, J. (1999). Analyzing interaction patterns in dysfunctional teams, *Small Group Research*, 30(4): 491–518.

Kiefer, T. and Barclay, L.J. (2012). Understanding the mediating role of toxic emotional experiences in the relationship between negative emotions and adverse outcomes, *Journal of Occupational and Organizational Psychology*, 85(4): 600–25.

Mahlendorf, M.D. (2015). Allowance for failure: reducing dysfunctional behaviour by innovating accountability practices, *Journal of Management & Governance*, 19(3): 655–86.

Maruping, L.M., Viswanath, V. and Thatcher, S.M. (2015). Folding under pressure or rising to the occasion? Perceived time pressure and the moderating role of team temporal leadership, *Academy of Management Journal*, 58(5): 1313–33.

Mintzberg, H. (1973). *The Nature of Managerial Work*. New York: Harper & Row.

Mintzberg, H. (1990). The manager's job: folklore and fact, *Harvard Business Review*, 68(2): 163–76.

Nansubuga, F., Munene, J.C. and Ntayi, J.M. (2015). Can reflection boost competences development in organisations?, *European Journal of Training and Development*, 39(6): 504–21. http://dx.doi.org/10.1108/EJTD-01-2015-0004.

Santos, C.M. and Passos, A.M. (2013). Team mental models, relationship conflict and effectiveness over time, *Team Performance Management*, 19(7/8): 363–85.

Senge, P.M. (1990). *The Fifth Discipline: The Art and Practice of Learning Organizations*. London: Random House Business Books.

Smith, I. M. and Brummel, B.J. (2013). Investigating the role of the active ingredients in executive coaching, *Coaching: An International Journal of Theory, Research and Practice*, 6(1): 57–71. DOI:10.1080/17521882.2012.758649.

Van Fleet, D. and Griffin, R.W. (2015). Dysfunctional organization culture: the role of leadership in motivating dysfunctional work behaviors, *Journal of Managerial Psychology*, 21(8): 698–708.

Yang, I. (2015). The positive outcomes of 'Socially Sharing Negative Emotions' in work teams: a conceptual exploration, *European Management Journal*, 34(2): 172–81.

Yang, M.-Y., Cheng, F.-C. and Chuang, A. (2015). The role of affects in conflict frames and conflict management, *International Journal of Conflict Management*, 26(4): 427–49.

Zoltan, R. (2015). Group dynamics and team functioning in an organisational context, *Ecoforum*, 4(2): 154–8.

Psychology references

Maslow, A.H. (1954) *Motivation and Personality*. New York: Harper and Row.

Rogers, C. (1951) *Client-Centered Therapy: Its Current Practice, Implications, and Theory*. London: Constable.

Seligman, M.E.P. (2011) *Flourish: A New Understanding of Happiness and Wellbeing and How to Achieve Them*. London: Nicholas Brealey Publishing.

Seligman, M.E.P. (2011) *Flourish: A Visionary New Understanding of Happiness and Wellbeing*. New York: Free Press.

6 Demands on manager and team leader

Summary

Line managers and team leaders carry the burden of delivering organizational strategy through to the individuals in their charge. In addition, multiple external authorities (CIPD, Chartered Management Institute (CMI), Institute of Leadership and Management (ILM)) inform us that line managers and team leaders are also best placed to deal with the personal development of these individuals. This developmental role is often not seen as being the responsibility of the line manager or team leader; there is more a preference to devolve this task to the training department or the human resource manager partner. Where this is the case, the organization and the individuals concerned will be placed at a disadvantage, with many valuable learning opportunities missed and overlooked. Therefore if the line managers and team leaders accept this role of development of their wards too, we are fortunate indeed. This chapter explores the ability of the line manager or team leader to wear these various hats and deliver to the ever-expanding list that seems to fall on their desk.

Keywords: management environment, manager expectations, employee expectations

Introduction

Aside from the challenging VUCA environment (volatility, uncertainty, complexity, ambiguity) and having to do more with less resource, these are possibly the tip of the iceberg of demands made of our line managers and team leaders. The change element alone, coupled with the VUCA environment, was highlighted 23 times during the interviews, as captured in the following statement:

> I think a key challenge is change. There's always change – no matter how big or small it is, it still affects people.

The time element (reviewed earlier) was strongly linked to change, as reflected in this manager's statement:

> Very often the challenge as a manager in today's world, I would say, is finding the time so they're not completely reactive to change and they can be more proactive.

This further adds to the ambiguity and expansion of demands placed on the line manager, team leader and team members who are trying to be timely and proactive within the change environment; this was strongly referenced as *perpetual change, rapid change, unexpected change* and *constant change*.

Aims

Having established that teams are recognized as a necessary structure for business success and with change regarded as a routine part of operational practice (Figure 6.1), it really does create an added layer of complexity to the challenging environment for managers. This chapter captures the demands being placed on managers and team leaders as an appreciation of the pressures they are dealing with on a daily basis.

The new team environment

Another kind of change reported by the interviewed managers and leaders was that of status change within a team (Driskell et al. 2017). This includes the broadening or extending of an individual's role to fill perceived resource gaps, which may result in some roles becoming more relevant while others become discarded. This is commonplace in the compressed roles as witnessed when layers of management are removed. Compression of management can lead to issues such as a change to the strategic core roles creating disruption in team coordination and performance. This is reflected in the captured statements from the managers and team leaders such as *changing dynamics,*

Figure 6.1 Impact of change

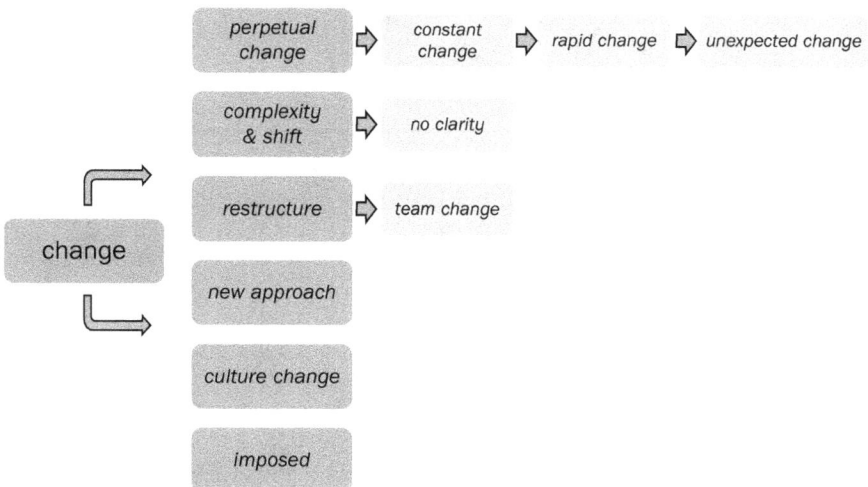

changing relationships, changing roles and *positional power*, all of which can create challenge individually and collectively within the team, especially when occurring at a pace. To illustrate the impact of status change, the following story was related by a company director who was employed as an executive coach to the CEO, and now reports to the same CEO as an employee within the organization:

> Now, the boot is completely on the other foot. He is now my boss. He knows everything and I know nothing; I am floundering around. It's now very difficult and challenging. It's also been the lack of certainty about my own position, namely 'let's see how it goes over the next 6 months'. I have had a number of meltdowns. I don't know whose team I am in, what team I am in, what my contribution is.

From this account, change can be seen to have affected personal well-being and performance. In a constant change environment of non-standard employment arrangements (Akron et al. 2016), flatter structures (Amos and Klimoski 2014) and greater reliance on potentially transient project teams (and therefore individuals, disrupting the social connection element mentioned), the high incidence of change references reported by the managers and leaders appear to be driven primarily from outside the team. The impact of change outside of team management control was viewed as negative, such as *redundancies, restructuring, enforced job rotation, environmental change, regulatory change, transferred staff, staff feeling threatened by change, insecurity, intimidated by change.* For these reasons, Bradley et al. (2012) reported that team leadership and line management are replacing divisional, unit leadership and management structures to ensure the requisite monitoring and support of staff to reduce worker uncertainty and drive delivery within required time frames. This need for refocusing staff and offering constant confirmation are the realities of an ever-changing, uncertain and volatile environment.

A canvas for conflict

There do seem to be more pressing daily challenges that evolve because of this context. For example in 2008, 85 per cent of employees across Europe dealt with some form of daily conflict, with the average employee spending 2.1 hours a week dealing with conflict. This represents 370 million days lost every year in the UK (CIPD 2020; Bradley et al. 2012).

In the 2020 report cited by the CIPD (Chen et al. 2012), conflict was very much a part of organizational life. The situation does not seem to have improved in over a decade, with conflict being a common occurrence at work according to a significant proportion of both employees (26 per cent) and employers (20 per cent). The survey of employees found that just over a third (35 per cent) had experienced some form of interpersonal conflict over the past year

Table 6.1 Conflict categories

Conflict category from Interviews

conflict within team	culture (12)	different value base
arguments	pulled in all directions	lack of guidance
tensions	habits	talking behind back
people being different	standards create tension	gender
different characters	traditions	politics
no cohesion (2)	bad behaviour	friction – workload
boundary issues (2)	oversensitive staff	bad behaviours and attitudes
discord (3)	different personalities and ways of working	not sharing
entrenched ways	team members holding different opinions	angry staff
disagreement	staff who do not belong	jealousy
mixed abilities	upsetting comments	heated discussions
diverse personalities	criticism	different skills sets

Numbers in brackets are for those items mentioned multiple times during the interviews.

at work, either as an isolated dispute or an ongoing difficult relationship. From the 30 interviews conducted for this book, Table 6.1 captures what the managers reported as being the conflict areas that they were required to deal with on a regular basis.

Cultural conflict was reported 12 times, boundary issues reported twice along with no cohesion, and finally discord was reported three times. All the other items listed in this table capture the contributory issues reported from the 30 interviews, providing a grim picture of the lot of the line manager or team leader in the current work environment. It is worthy of note that this analysis was made during pre-pandemic times; the pandemic may have exacerbated some of these reported conflict areas and the managers' challenge.

If the manager or team leader does not intervene where conflict is bubbling, competition for dominance from extrovert team members may counteract the ability of the team to resolve a task conflict in a productive manner (Lin et al. 2017). This observation is supported by the data from the interviews as conflict arising from *different characters, jealousy, team members holding different opinions* and *diverse personalities.* Some facets of extraversion can precipitate dysfunctional conflict, especially where there are *oversensitive staff* members in a team, as represented in the data as *different personalities and ways of working, entrenched ways, disagreements, criticism, boundary issues, arguments, tensions* and *politics*. For these reasons, the method for handling and solving staff interpersonal conflict matters a great deal and contributes to securing organizational long-term objectives (Al-Nasser and Mohamed 2015). The line managers and team leaders interviewed also reported that this was not a task to be devolved to anyone else. It squarely lands as their personal responsibility to address the issues, with the support and expectation of team members.

Habits, traditions and *entrenched ways of doing things* may lead team members to approach activities with *differing skill sets* and *mixed ability*, resulting in *lack of cohesion* leading to *friction* and *arguments between team members*. The provoker of this tension within a team may become the focus of *criticism* with *upsetting comments, talking behind one's back* and potentially with some *heated discussion*. These factors are evidently not conducive to a functioning team or to enhancing relationships. While the findings from established authors summarized in the team effectiveness models (Table 3.1) remain valid, there are additional insights to be gained from these interviews which specifically address the primary challenges relating to bad attitude and conflict within teams. The next section presents the interview data on challenging attitudes.

Challenging attitudes

The following scenario from one of the interviewed managers and team leaders illustrates the impact an individual attitude can have:

> To be honest we had a member of the team who really didn't want to be there. He just wasn't enjoying his job, and everybody would call him Happy Jazz, because he was so miserable... and he used to get such bad publicity and that would come back to the rest of the team. I had to sit down with him and go through numerous discussions with him about how he dealt with people, how he was...

Many of the managers interviewed mentioned certain attitudes which fall within the descriptors of the dysfunctional behaviour categories previously reviewed in Chapter 5. Table 6.2 lists the characteristics of attitudinal challenges reported by the managers or team leaders within the various categories of unproductive or dysfunctional behaviours (Table 5.1), plus associated academic research references from recent publications. This offers further evidence of the new environment managers and team leaders are having to address.

The importance of attitude on the *tone* of the team can have a measurable impact (Chen et al. 2012) where under *negative team affective tone*, efforts of the team members are less likely to promote team cooperation (as in the scenario of Happy Jazz above) due to a preoccupation with emotional regulation and distractions preventing them from pursuing team goals. Team affective tone not only affects team effectiveness but can also influence contributory factors such as team reputation, which potentially explains why attitude and conflict were reported as key challenges by the managers interviewed. Attitude and conflict situations were the most reported challenges in this data, with 38 and 51 reports respectively. A sample of the reported attitudinal challenges related to behaviour from one manager/leader is cited below:

> *Those who do not perform, bad and negative behavioural attitudes, behaving defensively or super protectionism...*

Resulting in conflict and mediocrity in the team. *Bad attitude*, *bullies* and *toxic staff* can impact negatively on the behaviour of the whole team, observable as negative team affective tone (Kaufmann 2012). Similarly, Lin et al. (2017) have noted that workplace bullying involves repetitive, inappropriate, tenacious negative behaviour (whether verbal, physical or otherwise) directed to a specific target or individual team member by one or more people, and is a form of social aggression, hostility and antisocial behaviour in an organizational or team setting. Such behaviour was reported repeatedly by the interviewed managers as representative of *conflict within the team*, the inference being that this behaviour undermines the ability of the target person(s) to work effectively and thereby impacting team cohesion, collaboration and team output.

Table 6.2   Attitudinal challenge

Category	Examples from interviewees	Supporting established research (although no solution offered)
poor communication preventing team effectiveness (supported by 13 interviewees)	bad attitude	**Jurkiewicz and Giacalone 2016** dysfunctional cultures can directly endorse misconduct
	reluctance	
	resistance (2)	
	negative attitude (2)	
	sabotage (3)	
	out of control	
	defensive	
	not willing to change	
	not rational	
	non-reactive	
	ranting and raving	
	over controlling	
	not willing	

(Continued)

Table 6.2 (Continued)

Category	Examples from interviewees	Supporting established research (although no solution offered)
does not take responsibility for disruptive actions / behaviour (supported by 8 interviewees)	discontented undermining (3) acting like a child bullies antagonistic maverick personalities bad feelings toxic staff	**Kaufmann 2012** challenge arises when disagreements are allowed to manifest in the form of interpersonal conflict that spirals into a dysfunctional working relationship and impedes collaboration
threatening if allowed to spiral (supported by 11 interviewees)	nastiness frustration lack of respect being kept in dark unhappy staff defensive when lack of understanding devious championing own agenda block progress task avoidance behaviour – bothersome	**Chen et al. 2012** conflict is the most common social phenomenon in organizations leading to friction between employees, conflict among departments, confrontation among organizations which threaten development. Interpersonal conflict is important and has great impact on staff relationships at work conflict can lead to compromised job satisfaction, reduced motivation, lack of engagement and low employee performance

Poor or bad attitude is the fuel that leads to conflict situations (Kozlowski and Bell 2003, cited in Ehrhardt et al. 2013; Vincent-Hoper et al. 2012), which are described as unproductive and wreaking havoc on organizational performance (Phipps et al. 2013). The interviewed line managers and team leaders revealed that this type of attitude typically starts with a disagreement or misunderstanding. Problem and conflict avoidance are not the solution, as the corollary is that any resultant negativity can make the target team member feel uncomfortable or intimidated, resulting in a negative team tone (Shahid and Shahid 2013) which we have established is not conducive to team effectiveness. Where there is team conflict, team members will decide to work either in opposition or in isolation rather than collectively, with the resultant impact on the team being dysfunctional behaviour. Increased appreciation concerning conflict further endorses these observations along with the changing environment many modern-day managers and team leaders are expected to operate in.

Expectation of the manager or team leader

Leaders and managers play a vital role in determining team outcomes and culture across all types of teams (Amos and Klimoski 2014) and functions. The fact that culture can have such an impact on a team is supported by other observers affirming that organizational culture plays an important role in organizational growth and development and can substantially impact organizational performance (Kivipõld 2015). Since the expected organizational infrastructure is the team, the importance the line manager or team leader may have in developing the correct team culture cannot be denied. The importance of correct leadership in this environment cannot be underestimated when pointing to the capability of the line manager or team leader as a knowledge coordinator with the potential to impact different stakeholders (Amos and Klimoski 2015). This requires exemplary leadership behaviour to encourage teamwork, typically including the initiation of the appropriate team structure, goal setting and consideration of individual skills and capabilities within the team (Gerard et al. 2017). This is an impossible deliverable for any line manager or team leader without spending the time to get to know individual team members.

In addition, where leaders take into consideration the individual skills and capabilities of team members, it is observed that sustainable outcomes are achieved more often in organizations where employees are engaged, motivated and healthy and where organizational performance exists as a central focus to their function (Yang et al. 2015). This may be dependent on the cohesion that is perceived throughout the organization, since negative feelings are recorded as inhibiting social integration and cohesion (Vincent-Hoper et al. 2012). Line managers and team leaders positively influence the team for greater effort by communicating effectively about shared goals and values, and setting an example of the required behaviour while attaining peak performance from their team members (Kivipõld 2015). The importance of line managers and team leaders in fostering team sharing is critical and apparently reliant on their ability to leverage tacit and implicit knowledge through engaging team members. One expert defines knowledge accumulation, sharing and creation as a central issue in knowledge management and knowledge transfer between team members. These issues all need to be coordinated or be engineered by management activities and leadership behaviour including knowledge of exchange collaboration (Ehrhardt et al. 2013).

Fostering collaboration

Collaboration was earlier identified as a team success factor (Fairhurst and Connaughton 2014) which is reliant on active associated knowledge sharing that occurs within a team. Complex team structures rely heavily on highly skilled individuals to share socially and technically with line managers and team leaders addressing this new norm of complexity, irrationality and continuous change in teams by adopting a communication-centred approach (Ehrhardt et al. 2013).

As previously reaffirmed via public reports and authors (Hall 2013), communication (including that communicated subliminally via line manager or team leader behaviour) becomes a conduit of and for the desired behavioural outcome and a transmission channel for the message of the desired direction. To underline the importance of the management and leadership communication skills, there is supported evidence that teams will be committed, or rather can commit, when they understand their shared purpose (Sun et al. 2017). Sincere, demonstrated and aligned communication (Gerard et al. 2017) creates a dynamic connection between actions, meaning and context (Peng and Lin 2016), enabling a comprehension, engagement and connection with the tasks and goals for team members. Some experts claim that organizations need to stop considering line managers and team leadership as a control function and instead focus on dialogue and mutual interdependency between managers, leaders and their followers (Peng and Lin 2016). Additional experts further highlight the importance of communication, both verbal and observed, as a vital element of the social experience that motivates subordinates when referring to the nature and frequency of informal day-to-day communication between line manager, team leaders and subordinates (Fairhurst and Connaughton 2014). Others posit that achieving this type of motivational communication is due to the line manager or team leader not just managing meaning but also managing the receptors of the meaning (Phipps et al. 2013). This echoes the PERMA model from Seligman as reviewed in addition to linking to the internalization of commitment (Fairhurst and Connaughton 2014).

This deeply connecting type of communication is relational, without bias and enables trust building (Hall 2013). Communication of this quality and level facilitated by the team line manager or team leader can become an engine for change (Auer et al. 2014) through encouraging mutual understanding between team members and the provision of a visible reference to guide expectation and standards.

The required competencies, skills and abilities, along with the desire and the time investment from the line manager and team leader, offer a possible means of achieving the required team results and total collaboration of every team member.

In the following chapter we shall explore the ability of the line manager and team leader to foster communication standards through the application of a coaching approach, via *manager as coach*.

Psychological underpinning

In this psychological section, we shall apply the potential of managing with the support of personal construct psychology, referred to as PCP (George Kelly). PCP started life as a therapeutic intervention to assist an individual's progress and is based on 11 behavioural patterns.

Maybe you have seen or heard the statement *when you believe you can, you can*; this is a perfect example of PCP. However, for the case of a line manager or team leader, their activities include assisting the belief, supporting resources, bolstering skills, achieving the team vision and enabling individual team members to attain and believe the required psychological construct. Once this construct is formed in the individual's mind, they can achieve whatever they wish.

From a personality psychologist perspective, our mind is critical to our personality through controlling our interaction with others, how we respond in situations and contexts, and how we may respond to questions. Therefore, if we achieve personal awareness of how we react and respond to others, we can manage how we achieve alignment within our team. If we do not have this awareness, the foundations for conflict could become evident. This awareness is akin to emotional intelligence, as focused on by Edmondson in the comparison and summary of team effectiveness models (Table 8.2).

The role of the line manager or team leader in facilitating this alignment and engagement towards achieving team goals may require a true understanding and appreciation of the key drivers and capability that each member brings to the team.

The PCP pathway to alignment has several stages:

1 facilitative conversations
2 using metaphors to anchor the mind on the desired goal
3 knowing your team members and creating individual drivers – from a PCP perspective, this would be achieved through use of a dyad, dependency and implication grid to enhance appreciation of their challenge and required area of focus
4 attainment can be verified via psychological measures
5 task analysis will ensure all elements are covered successfully
6 enabling the team member to perform the required task on behalf of the team

These stages may be a natural mode of operation for some line managers and team leaders, although not all will pursue facilitative conversations apart from when conducting a periodic appraisal process. This may well be too late to enable an individual to achieve and deliver their goals on time if this activity is based on a protracted time basis.

Personal construct psychology can be a powerful tool when applied in the sports arena and does appear to have a useful application for teams and organizations. It does though require engagement from the line manager or team leader to add value for the team.

Case study

Eleanor had been in post about five years in a massive organization of more than 2000 staff, which meant some colleagues still considered her as 'new' simply due to not having had an opportunity to work with her to date.

A new project evolved which Eleanor's line manager knew she would be perfect to lead and that she had the right knowledge and skill set to do so. The landscape was that two other staff members had identified the issue that created the new project opportunity and had outlined this to the line manager in a report seeking funding to address it. They were successful in securing funds to support the project but didn't have the time or skills themselves to carry out or lead the solution required.

Eleanor's line manager asked her to apply for the project lead since this played to her skills, and through being seconded for the duration of the project she was able to deliver within the time frame (which was challenging). In addition, Eleanor had the network to support its delivery, as well as the knowledge.

After applying and being interviewed as to her plans for the project, Eleanor got the job and set to planning immediately, creating a flow chart of all the activities required and the touch points to understand the scope of the task in hand, pulling the team members together and setting logistics in place. Multiple meetings and activities revolved around this project and time was tight. A quick briefing meeting was carried out at the outset and Eleanor was provided with the original report as a starting point, which outlined the aims and objectives. The briefing meeting offered internal contacts that may be of assistance, but no other details were shared.

It was not until two months into the project that Eleanor learned that one of the report originators had put some logistical elements in place. This created huge issues of duplication, but also explained why Eleanor had been getting resistance from some team members, who had not mentioned the earlier iteration of any plans. Now knowing they had been given different instructions earlier from someone who was not the project leader, maybe they felt unsure as to what reaction they would get from Eleanor. The result was wasted time, energy and effort putting in place a process that was not ideal, and changes were difficult and too late to correct. All the materials Eleanor had created supported the process plans she had made but the processes had been set up differently on the instruction of a non-expert in the field required for the desired outputs. Eleanor did check status with her line manager, who confirmed it was her role to lead the project, because these situations make you doubt yourself as leader, don't they?

The stakeholders were confused, time was wasted and consequently the result was not as good as it could have been, as being two months into the project and working to a tight schedule didn't allow for major changes.

Eleanor always felt as though she had been handed a 'poisoned chalice', and even though the project was delivered on time, along with offering some fabulous personal insights, it is not a project she looks back on with pride.

Whatever the drivers, there was no cohesion or collaboration in this handover and the lack of trust impeded communication, which didn't facilitate the results that could have made better use of the secured funds.

Reflective questions

- What changes have my team experienced as part of work recently, either actual or anticipated? What sort of disruption is this creating from what I can see or hear? What might I be missing? What climate or tone might this be creating in my team?
- What changes have individuals in my team experienced, either actual or anticipated, at work or at home? What sort of inequalities might this person have experienced in life or in work? What sort of pressures is this creating for them, in their shoes, today? How might that taint their experience of work, today? What might that tell me about how to respond to this person, today or tomorrow?
- What habits appear to be useful in my teams, and in what way are they useful? What habits appear to be unhelpful for wider team performance or well-being? What role might they be serving for the team, or individuals within it?
- What attitudes appear in my teams? What effects do they seem to create in my teams? What might I be missing which generates those attitudes or gives them permission to persist?
- What other facilitative conversations might be useful to create supportive environments? Where and when could I hold these to be sensitive to others' and my own needs?
- What metaphors might be useful to use to anchor the mind on the desired goal rather than historical, current or future problems? What metaphors do my teams, and the individuals within them, use and what do they say about how the teams see their roles and how they should be working together?
- To what extent might a task analysis help clarify the nature of roles and their distribution across teams?
- How might I be supporting or hindering collaboration within and across my teams? What do your teams say about collaboration within and across teams? To what extent do I acknowledge and attempt to address this, or permit the current set of behaviours?

References

Akron, S., Feinblit, O., Hareli, S. and Tzafrir, S.S. (2016). Employment arrangements diversity and work group performance, *Team Performance Management*, 22(5/6): 310–30. http://dx.doi.org/10.1108/TPM-11-2015-0053.

Al-Nasser, A. and Mohamed, B. (2015). Examining the relationship between organizational coaching and workplace counterproductive behaviours in the United Arab Emirates, *International Journal of Organizational Analysis*, 23(3): 378–403. DOI: 10.1108/IJOA-08-2014-0793.

Amos, B. and Klimoski, R.J. (2014). Courage: making teamwork work well, *Group & Organization Management*, 39(1): 110–28. DOI: 10.1177/1059601113520407.

Auer, J.C., Kao, C.-Y., Hemphill, L., Johnston, E.W. and Teasley, S.D. (2014). The uncertainty challenge of contingent collaboration, *Human Resource Management Journal*, 24(4): 531–47.

Bradley, B.H., Klotz, A.C., Postlethwait, B.E. and Brown, K.G. (2012). Ready to rumble: how team personality composition and task conflict interact to improve performance, *Journal of Applied Psychology*, 98(2): 385–92. DOI: 10.1037/a0029845.

Chen, X.H., Zhao, K., Liu, X. and Wu, D.D. (2012). Improving employees' job satisfaction and innovation performance using conflict management, *International Journal of Conflict Management*, 23(2): 151–72.

CIPD (Chartered Institute of Personnel and Development) (2020). *Managing Conflict in the Modern Workplace*. London: CIPD. Available at: https://www.cipd.co.uk/knowledge/fundamentals/relations/disputes/managing-workplace-conflict-report (accessed 23 January 2023).

Driskell, T., Salas, E. and Driskell, J.E. (2017). Teams in extreme environments: alterations in team development and teamwork, *Human Resource Management Review*, 28(4): 434–49. http://dx.doi.org/10.1016/j.hrmr.2017.01.002.

Ehrhardt, K., Miller, J.S., Freeman, S.J. and Hom, P.W. (2013). Examining project commitment in cross-functional teams: antecedents and relationship with team performance, *Journal of Business and Psychology*, 29(3): 443–61. DOI: 10.1007/s10869-013-9325.

Fairhurst, G. and Connaughton, S.L. (2014). Leadership: a communication perspective, *Leadership*, 10(1): 7–35. DOI: 10.1177/1742715013509396.

Gerard, L., McMillan, J. and D'Annunzio-Green, N. (2017). Conceptualising sustainable leadership, *Industrial and Commercial Training*, 49(3): 116–26.

Hall, J.L. (2013). Managing teams with diverse compositions: implications for managers from research on the faultline model, *Advanced Management Journal*, 78(1): 4–10.

Jurkiewicz, C.L. and Giacalone, R.A. (2016). Organizational determinants of ethical dysfunctionality, *Journal of Business Ethics*, 136(1): 1–12. DOI: 10.1007/s10551-014-2344-z.

Kaufmann, B. (2012). The anatomy of dysfunctional working relationships, *Business Strategy Series*, 13(2): 102–6.

Kivipõld, K. (2015). Organizational leadership capability – a mechanism of knowledge coordination for inducing innovative behaviour. A case study in Estonian service industries, *Baltic Journal of Management*, 10(4): 478–96. DOI: 10.1108/BJM-10-2014-0152.

Lin, C.-P., He, H., Baruch, Y. and Ashforth, B.E. (2017). The effects of team affective tone on team performance: the roles of team identification and team cooperation, *Human Resource Management*, 56(6): 931–52.

Peng, J.C. and Lin, J. (2016). Linking supervisor feedback environment to contextual performances: the mediating effect of leader–member exchange, *Leadership & Organization Development Journal*, 37(6): 802–20.

Phipps, S.T.A., Prieto, L.C. and Ndinguri, E.N. (2013). Understanding the impact of employee involvement on organizational productivity: the moderating role of organizational commitment, *Journal of Organizational Culture, Communications and Conflict*, 17(2): 107–20.

Shahid, A. and Shahid, M. (2013). Gaining employee commitment: linking to organisational effectiveness, *Journal of Management Research*, 5(1): 250.

Sun, H., Pei-Lee, T. and Karis, H. (2017). Team diversity, learning, and innovation: a mediation model, *Journal of Computer Information Systems*, 57(1): 22–30.

Vincent-Hoper, S., Muser, C. and Janneck, M. (2012). Transformational leadership, work engagement and occupational success, *Career Development International*, 17(7): 663–82.
Yang, M.-Y., Cheng, F.-C. and Chuang, A. (2015). The role of affects in conflict frames and conflict management, *International Journal of Conflict Management*, 26(4): 427–49.

Psychology reference

Kelly, G.A. (1955/1991). *The Psychology of Personal Constructs*, Volume 1. London: Routledge.

7 The coaching approach

Summary

This chapter outlines the research findings related to the experience of the interviewed line managers and team leaders in dealing with team challenge. It reinforces and validates the landscape reports (from CIPD, CMI and ILM) that line managers and team leaders are best placed to develop team members and address team challenge. But it is also recognized that this may not be a role every line manager or team leader will feel comfortable with. This chapter explores the evolution of the emergence of manager as coach (MAC) or coach-like leadership as the approach adopted by the interviewed managers and leaders and draws on their advice and insight in dealing with the demands of a modern team utilizing a coaching approach.

Keywords: manager as coach, mindset, coaching approach to team challenge, evolution of manager as coach/coach-like leader

Introduction

A manager who employs coaching to lead their team is referred to as a *manager as coach* (MAC). MAC is defined as a manager or leader with coaching experience likely to facilitate employee learning and development to best influence positive team behaviour (Ellinger et al. 2006). Due to the multiple demands (Tocan and Chindris-Vasiou 2013; Suriyankietkaew 2013; Fairhurst and Connaughton 2014; Pousa and Mathieu 2015) being placed upon teams (Driskell et al. 2017) in the VUCA environment, it becomes evident a new management paradigm is required (Vincent-Hoper et al. 2012; Hall 2013; Kivipõld 2015) with an emphasis on constructive and developmental feedback (Fairhurst and Connaughton 2014). This also supports the assertion from the CIPD that highlighted line managers or team leaders as being best placed to address such developmental needs of their team members. This trend is reminiscent of the operational team framework from the previously reviewed team models, where learning is listed for improving employee work performance and the need to cope with the constant change experienced in a modern business environment.

Aims

Manager as coach (MAC) and the use of coaching by internal line managers and team leaders is a consequence of the VUCA environment in conjunction with organizations seeking to leverage talent and specific desired behaviours (such as flexibility, listening and sharing with colleagues). This demands a new paradigm for improving team support *in the moment* to deliver organizational goals in an efficient and timely manner (Batson and Yoder 2012). This context lies in addition to the delayering and flatter structures within organizations, which means stepping up, taking responsibility and assisting colleagues is also expected. This chapter outlines why a coaching approach is so popular, and the benefits of applying coaching to achieve the desired results of a fully functioning team. In addition, the chapter explores the demands being placed upon line managers and team leaders to develop their team members while delivering the organizational goals.

Why coaching?

A primary objective of organizational coaching is to enable people to work together by initiating conversations that generate alignment (Al-Nasser and Mohamed 2015). This certainly makes sense when we appreciate how we rely on team members to work cooperatively and seamlessly to meet timelines and output demands. Other experts support this view, stating that line managers and team leaders are a vital cog in the wheel of assisting organizations to achieve sustainability through a dialogue-focused leadership, with greater reflection and a participative leadership style (Gerard et al. 2017). The intent and purpose of a coaching style of leadership are to achieve these positive outcomes: dialogue, reflection (for learning), and improved individual and team participation. Coaching has evolved from a task-focused process to a robust leadership concept with an additional psychosocial behavioural focus (Zoltan 2015) essential for the participation desired in team working. The need to develop self-efficacy and the promotion of employee empowerment results in organizations turning to coaching to support their goal achievement. A CIPD survey in 2013 on hierarchical coaching (as for MAC coaching subordinate team members) found coaching by line managers or team leaders to be the second most effective form of learning within teams. This observation of the increased use of coaching by line managers and team leaders was reiterated as being one of the most prominent activities that appropriately serves the learning and development needs of human resource development (Cox et al. 2014). Recently, the skills and expertise of the team manager using coaching were referred to as coach-like leadership, which includes similar characteristics such as reflection and asking good questions (Karaçivi and Demirel 2014).

The evidence for this evolution and the need for line managers and team leaders to employ a coaching style has gathered traction. This starts with the premise that line managers and team leaders can and should be role models for the expected behaviours specific to their organization, and for orchestrating the learning of tasks and skills required in specific work-related settings (Anderson 2013). Who better to do this than the team leaders and line managers in that work-related context? The MAC and coach-like leader is also expected to be emotionally intelligent and requires an in-depth appreciation of the team members they manage and lead. Managing and leading in a coaching way requires a more personal-focused approach. Since team leaders and managers carry out the same role *in essence*, flipping from one to the other (i.e. leading and managing) as dictated by the context, it could be argued that these team-facing roles (managing and leading) need to be administered with emotional intelligence. This personal characteristic of the team leader or manager is also highlighted and defined in Edmondson's team effectiveness model through the manager or team leader being self-aware and having the ability to self-regulate, to motivate themselves and their followers, and be socially adept (Engelbrecht et al. 2014). This is a foundational requirement for any manager or team leader who employs coaching. Interestingly, many human resource managers note that when a leader or manager attends a coaching course, they become more introspective. This self-reflection on their own adopted style can be revealing in itself and can bring about a change in their leadership or management style and their interaction with others.

Capability of managers and coach-like leaders to forge strong relationships

Some researchers in this area have also highlighted that workplace coaching is distinct from specialized coaching practices (Engelbrecht et al. 2014), while other observers champion the need for a good relationship as the platform for the line manager or team leader to fully support staff development (Anderson 2013). This manager/leader–team member relationship (Batson and Yoder 2012) and personal occupational self-efficacy (OSE) as a manager or team leader have been interpreted as predictive measures of managerial or leadership coaching behaviour and ultimate team success (Anderson 2013). This inclines line managers and team leaders to be empathetic to fulfil the requirements of relationship building with and among team members. Other experts also list coaching leaders as having reduced organizational politics, thus enabling fully functioning teams. This suggestion to keep pace with our changing environment requires an ability to *inspire* individual team members (by linking personal and organizational goals), *adapt* the communication and support required (performance to the collective needs of the team through clear work expectations and short-term goals), *align* team members and activities (by providing regular informal feedback) and *grow* the team members as well as one's self (developmental component of managerial work) (de Haan et al. 2013; Karaçivi and Demirel 2014).

Researchers of team effectiveness, Dello Russo et al. (2016), support the need for and the importance of a good relationship when focusing on the impact of leader–follower as a conduit for learning and a positive working alliance through carefully transmitting meaning and expected behavioural outcomes to team individuals. A positive working alliance improves the likelihood of coaching success and is an important element of coaching (Ewen et al. 2013; Fairhurst and Connaughton 2014) in any context, not excluding that of a MAC or a coach-like leader. Summarizing several of the required characteristics of a MAC or a coach-like leader starts with the first characteristic of role modelling, followed by promoting a sense of positive accountability for one's own actions (de Haan et al. 2013), removing obstacles for our team members, challenging when appropriate to facilitate progress and broadening the perspectives as may be required in a diverse team (Anderson 2013; Kim 2014). Role modelling is perhaps the most critical and empowering behaviour for any line manager or team leader to display (Katzenbach and Smith 1999). This is possibly even more true for a line manager or team leader who claims to adopt a coaching stance and as a result could be under constant scrutiny in carrying the responsibility to display the required standard of behaviour of a coach. The final characteristic is the provision of appropriate training for each team member, either directly or by identifying and providing resources for training as based on the foundational coaching principle of putting the development of others foremost. This training role of the MAC or coach-like leader accompanies the assertion that line managers and team leaders need to possess unbiased attitudes and beliefs, be open to communicate, readily appraise employees, challenge to prompt cognitive development in team members where appropriate, and provide and solicit timely feedback (Dahling et al. 2016). When observing, the MAC and coach-like leader need to facilitate and empower individual team members, to demonstrate belief in their employees, to learn enhancement processes and learn about their learners (Hagen and Peterson 2013). These characteristics are considered essential attributes of the MAC or coach-like leader, in addition to embracing the skills of asking powerful thought-provoking questions, listening carefully, providing direct communication and constructive feedback, creating and building trust between themselves and individual team members as well as between team members, creating awareness and appreciation of anything that is not aligned and interferes with team functioning, employing goal setting and acknowledging an accountability of process (Ellinger 2013, which underpins Hagen and Peterson 2013). This list can be quite challenging in itself for some line managers or coach-like leaders to deliver.

Managers and leaders with the right mindset

In its many iterations, coaching shares a common core, with its primary focus to improve performance by providing help to individuals, teams or organizations through a facilitative activity or intervention (Karaçivi and Demirel 2014). Line managers and team leaders are thought to be best placed to address such items of team development due to their constant contact with team members (Beattie et al. 2014). Line managers and team leaders can observe the contribution from every team member and are best able to establish significant links between each individual and the team performance (Clutterbuck 2013). Management and leadership modelling of the required contribution can facilitate increased commitment to the goals of the team, thus supporting the organizational outputs (Engelbrecht et al. 2014) and also contribute towards inspiring and motivating the team members. Furthermore, as individuals we can easily revert to our inclined way of doing things without the support of a proactive manager or inspiring leader to remind and assist us to maintain the required focus (Engelbrecht et al. 2014), thereby keeping the team on track. This tendency to revert and lapse into former approaches reinforces the responsibility of the MAC and coach-like leader to care for the development of others and highlights the importance of reflection as a learning tool. Without reflection, the line manager or team leader is unable to lead the team correctly or identify areas for improvements in team members or themselves (Kim et al. 2013).

Organizational managers, leaders and senior management also seek a less autocratic means of leveraging the best from their staff. This is achieved through inclusion, collaboration, participation and involvement as driven by the need for sustainability and the merging of middle management roles through delayering (Clutterbuck 2013), along with the increased pace of change demanding a more direct knowledge flow to enable the required reaction. Thus, this diminished distance between line managers and team leaders and their team members can foster increased engagement and committed staff, which will reap greater returns, individually and for the team (Nansubuga et al. 2015). Nevertheless, this will happen only if senior leaders trust and empower employees to do so. In parallel, there have been recent publications on the benefits of coaching in the workplace supporting the use of coaching for inclusive and effective decision-making plus offering a wider perspective for leading effectively (Agarwal et al. 2009). Senior managers cannot afford to miss out on valuable information feeds from their employees, and therefore need to embrace a coaching style for the health and growth of the organization. Coaching is described as a partnership process that guides an individual through their personal and professional development and creates alignment between the needs and intentions of the individual concerned and the organization (Belschak and Den Hartog 2010). How valuable could such insight be when building a motivated and enabled team.

Coaching therefore represents the required paradigm shift in managerial and leadership philosophy, challenging the leader-centric model of old in favour of greater reciprocity (Jones et al. 2016) and focusing on the workers towards total engagement. Managerial coaching and coach-like leadership have been credited with enabling line managers and team leaders to fulfil their role of developing staff, harnessing skills, improving knowledge and the ability of their team members to deliver an effective team and individual performance (Ciporen 2015). Coaching can also offer a continual informal development process (on the job, without down time) which is essential in a rapidly changing environment (Suriyankietkaew 2013). Line managers and team leaders possessing the right mindset to be able to adopt a coaching style *is essential* in the modern business environment. If they are unable or unwilling to coach by burying their own ego in favour of collaboration and team working, they are at risk of seriously damaging the possibilities achievable by their employees and the future of their organization. This can potentially lead to frustration for individual employees and multiple lost opportunities.

The following section discusses how management theorists and human resource experts conclude that coaching in a team has potential benefits if widely embraced, and offers a strong rationale for the approach of the MAC and coach-like leader to address team challenge.

Coaching approach to team challenge

Coaching can manage the complexity of co-working in a team setting (Anderson 2013) and support the requirement for the managerial and leadership paradigm. This allows for fast, sustainable, resilient responses based on proactive dialogue and achieving sustainability through fully engaged, focused employees providing individual motivation. The dialogue with the MAC or coach-like leader reinforces and refreshes the organizational goals as central to their activities (Dahling et al. 2016). The purpose of the MAC or coach-like leader in this context is to add value to the employees they lead and help them improve (Clutterbuck 2013), with coaching linked to employee engagement and work-related outcomes (Gerard et al. 2017). Coaching that revolves around effective goal setting and underpins alignment between the personal desires of employees and organizational needs is what defines the MAC or coach-like leader (Bommelje 2015). The actual task of achieving a specific goal can have a motivational effect on the individual achieving that goal, increasing their levels of self-efficacy and self-belief (Egan and Hamlin 2014) and having faith and confidence in their own ability. Once effective goal setting is accomplished, a coach would solicit feedback from the individual regarding progress and potential obstacles while expressing concern through a reflective dialogue to monitor their ability and comprehension, and identify areas where support may be required to accomplish their goals. If this model is adopted by the line manager or team leader, coaching can provide a constructive and robust framework for forward-focused solutions via thinking and driving personal development activities and offering a solid platform for stretched goals built on the success of the last achievement. Coaching as an intervention has to be effective as characterized by an open exchange and feedback between the line manager or team leader and their team members (Cheng et al. 2012; Fairhurst and Connaughton 2014; Karaçivi and Demirel 2014). In addition, the primary objective of organizational coaching is to enable and empower people to seek new possibilities for action, especially in terms of how they work individually, how they work collectively, how they collaborate and how they initiate a conversation that generates improved alignment towards their desired outcome (Bandura 2012). Employees who receive coaching appear to be more satisfied, more motivated and perceived as being more effective by their colleagues and other observers. Coaching of employees by line managers or team leaders has begun to be associated with higher productivity and increased profits and output (Dahling et al. 2016), with higher performance work teams tending to use coaching as their conduit to goal achievement.

Coaching is characterized by behavioural modelling. This is accomplished by the line manager or team leader modelling their own performance to illustrate to their team members appropriate examples of the activities and behaviours they should seek to follow (Al-Nasser and Mohamed 2015). This facilitates learning by enacting desired behaviours and observed performance (Kim et al. 2013). Coaching that is person-centred in addressing behavioural challenges with team individuals (Dahling et al. 2016) can be powerful when observed and monitored in others – especially the line manager or team leader (someone they want to have a constructive relationship with) observed by the targeted individual. This is a powerful behavioural change tool and reinforces the importance and potential impact of positive feedback through observing the modelled behaviour of managers and leaders. There are four actions within the scope and responsibility of the line manager or team leader when practising such modelling: 1) create a positive feedback environment, which is important if the individuals concerned can learn through having a conducive environment to absorb learning within; 2) create feedback within the whole team for the team as an entity to identify areas for improvement (as occurs in lean manufacturing teams), and realize where impediments may be and where improvements in the team process can be made; 3) identify sources of feedback for the team, offering practical examples to anchor the learning; 4) enable time to reflect and learn from their actions (Anderson 2013). One can appreciate how a coaching approach has the capacity to achieve an aligned workforce if these four actions are practised as a routine by the line manager or team leader.

Meaningful conversations

There are some critical elements that need to be in place between the line manager or team leader and employee to achieve personal reciprocal meaning-making conversations that are beneficial to both manager and team member (Al-Nasser and Mohamed 2015). This meaning-making is reliant on dialogue and reflection becoming commonplace through constructive coaching conversations. The MAC or coach-like leader has to be adept at meaning-making on an individual and team basis to *anchor* the task as important to the individual and other team members for delivery of the goal to be more assured. A consistent feature in the coaching literature is the importance of self-awareness by those involved in the coaching relationship (London and Mone 2015). This applies to line manager, team leader and team member where expectations of the line manager or team leader modelling the desired behaviours require a level of awareness of the potential impact they can have on their team (Anderson 2013). Team members also need to be aware of the impact they have on their team. Through a constructive, reflective coaching conversation with the line manager or team leader, this self-awareness can be fostered and shaped as required, while in a team the behaviour from and by all needs to support the team goals.

Many market reports (CIPD Learning and Talent Development Survey Report (2012), CMI in 2020, ILM) support earlier European Mentoring Coaching Council (EMCC) research in stating that the primary benefits of coaching are improved performance, increased motivation, team cohesion, staff retention and conflict resolution. Coaching-styled conversations can reduce ambiguities (through embedded challenging and reflective questioning techniques) and reduce tensions relating to potentially conflicting roles within a team, and have a positive effect on behaviour through reinforcing clarity of expectations (Passmore 2010; Anderson 2013). Coaching has been categorized as a simple framework for addressing challenge and influencing individuals while supporting sound decision-making behaviour in the context in which it occurs (Anderson 2013). In a fast-paced environment, having a trusted decision-making framework is valuable to all stakeholders, with the potential to save time and money. Robust decision-making can be referenced after the event to evidence non-bias and offer reassurance that all perspectives have been considered, through applying a coaching approach and questioning techniques. The context of workplace coaching is grounded in its specific occupational setting and is future-oriented and action-focused (Wakkee et al. 2010). It is therefore understandable why the line manager or team leader is best placed to address team challenge of any nature since they share the same context. The workplace is the place where adults learn how to become more efficient and effective. Coaching in the workplace assists the acquisition of this improved efficiency and effectiveness along with new skills, competencies and performance enhancement in terms of personal effectiveness, development, and personal and team growth (Hur et al. 2011).

The impact of coaching can be influential in how the MAC or coach-like leader affects relationships and demonstrates socio-emotional competence (Anderson 2013), which relates to the higher level of self-awareness referenced earlier (Bommelje 2015). The relationship between managerial, leadership coaching and team performance relies on a reflective dialogue which is key to improving individual and team performance (O'Broin and McDowall 2015). This dialogue develops a deeper understanding of an individual's behaviour (Karcivi and Demirel 2014) and its impact on personal and team performance (Buljac-Samardžić 2012; Schippers et al. 2013; Gerard et al. 2017), which facilitates opportunities for alignment of essential activities for successful, and potentially improved, team functioning. Reflection is integral to the coaching approach and is considered a new paradigm for practical knowing, acting and learning in a social situation like a work team environment (Hall 2013). Listening fully, asking critical questions and providing timely and constructive feedback forces each team member to stop and deliberate. This can be positive in itself but also has the potential to create conflict if the team members hold a different perspective on the issue at hand.

Being a role model

Relational and analytical skills, observation and rapport building are frequently cited as fundamental coaching skills for a line manager or a coach-like leader to adopt. If applied successfully, they can facilitate the avoidance of conflict. Coaching to manage stress in project teams is also recommended (Schippers et al. 2013), enabling the possibility of sharing and practising the adage of *a problem shared is a problem halved*. Whatever the elements responsible, talking through a challenge or a concern can often assist the individual to put the issue in perspective and gain new insights in how to address it, and allows an opportunity to stand back from it and make the scenario less stressful. Modelling and feedback can help team members understand what behaviours are necessary in unique contexts, how well they are doing when compared to the modelled behaviour and how well others are doing, while also appreciating the value of helping others for the benefit of the team (Nansubuga et al. 2015) and to support the required standards. Performance feedback drives results including those of setting clear expectations for employees, assisting problem-solving through having a preventative influence, providing work assignments that utilize team members' strengths and addressing development needs through regular, informal feedback (Berg and Karlsen 2013). These actions from the MAC or coach-like leader will support individual growth and team functioning to build a stronger organization.

Every one of these individual and team-enhancing feedback mechanisms can be applied by the MAC or coach-like leader to achieve team effectiveness and overcome potential conflict. To generate the greatest impact, constructive feedback requires a focus on strengths (to motivate and engage), to be accurate, to be timely and to be delivered by someone who knows the employee well. This will allow the individual to draw on examples and values known to be important and make the drivers for change resonate even more. This reinforces the MAC and coach-like leader as being well placed to observe and deliver the required feedback to the individuals they manage and lead. To be successful, there is a reliance on the line manager or team leader to create the right environment for the delivery and total acceptance of the feedback (Klein 2003, cited in London and Mone 2015). While developmental feedback may have social as well as task components, it is nevertheless important to illustrate how its impact can assist comprehension of the desired change. The manager or team leader does need to fully utilize these unique opportunities of shared context and observational feedback since *being in context* and *in the moment* with the team can have huge benefits for the individual's comprehension and for the team.

Conversely, the researcher Appelbaum devised a model (Appelbaum et al. 2000) referred to as AMO (Pulakos et al. 2012) where the *Ability* of the individual is considered, followed by clarification of the required expectations of them to *Motivate* and to seek *Opportunities* to fully apply their skills. This approach focuses on motivation through trust and the provision of ownership. From this simplistic model, the responsibility of the line manager and team leader to seek out opportunities and appropriate practice for their team members relies on knowing them well, and an awareness of their ability and what motivates them individually. Team members that take the time to reflect on their work processes and performance through facilitation with their MAC or coach-like leader can learn, correct and improve their performance (Peng and Lin 2016) and behaviour.

Importance of reflection

Reflection is recognized as an essential element of learning as it fosters focused discussion among different parties, which can lead to mutual learning, enhanced insight, deeper understanding of one another and the scenario, improved collaborative consciousness and corrective actions (Peng and Lin 2016). Reflection best benefits poorly performing teams (Appelbaum et al. 2000) since the greatest profit to be gained arises where there is the greatest potential for conflict in a team. A coaching approach can facilitate and create the necessary insight to encourage informative reflection. Reflection is known to be most valuable when team members are in a positive mindset, making them more conducive to the process of reflection, and when performance feedback is delivered accurately without bias or emotion (Schippers et al. 2013). This needs to take place within a safe environment specific to the learning required to create a favourable condition for positive assimilation of, for example, an analysis of required tasks. A positive feedback environment can improve task and organizational team performance and reduce deviant, counterproductive behaviour (Bommelje 2015; Nansubuga et al. 2015).

Such deviant behaviour has been identified as a potential root cause of dysfunctional team behaviour (Schippers et al. 2013). Coaching, though, has been referenced as a means of behavioural self-regulation (Kollée et al. 2013) with the provision of constructive ongoing feedback, assimilation of the required alignment and the need for alert observation from line managers and team leaders (Keyton 1999; Aquila 2007; Kaufmann 2012; Kiefer and Barclay 2012; Peng and Lin 2016). Managerial and leadership coaching is pivotal to team functioning and, being a reciprocal process, takes place in complex and demanding contexts where line managers and team leaders must motivate, improve and provide opportunities for team members to utilize their skills, expert knowledge and unique attributes. The facilitation of this exercise provides an ideal opportunity for the team member to absorb and embed this learning opportunity while acknowledging the pressure and responsibility for the MAC or coach-like leader to create the necessary condition for each team member to flourish.

The creation of a positive feedback environment is an essential requirement for effective coaching per se and within a team context. It requires an acceptance of mutuality between the MAC or coach-like leader and the team member, and the acknowledgement of a process of positive interaction over a sustained period of time. This process of interaction generates the potential for mutual understanding and the opportunity for the line manager or coach-like leader to challenge the values and attitudes of specific team members to achieve the necessary alignment of the team and the organization (Lin 2015). Although managerial and coach-like leadership is increasingly advocated in organizations, the function and context of leadership and management are distinct from specialized coaching (Ehrhardt et al. 2013) which can result in a further challenge, or even conflict, for some line managers and team leaders to deliver (Braun et al. 2013). The demanding expectations associated with the coaching approach are investigated below.

Demands on the MAC and coach-like leader

The language and intent of the team effectiveness models cited previously are representative of the language of coaching as based on social interaction (Anderson 2013) and provide substantive support to the MAC and the coach-like leader approach. Fleishman (1992) and Hackman (2002) refer to coaching as part of the requirement for team success. Organizations require their line managers and team leaders to improve the skills and motivation of team members to exert effort, and provide the necessary job opportunities to exploit their individual capabilities, knowledge and attributes (EMCC 2018). Line managers and team leaders are further expected to enable workers to accept ongoing change, to settle and condition employees to change by providing conducive surroundings, and to add value through support of individual members and functioning of the team (Peng and Lin 2016). The list of demands requires line managers and team leaders to acquire and practise new skills when interacting with employees (Anderson 2013; Dahling et al. 2016) and particularly the softer skills that may not be natural for some team leaders and line managers. However, these are a priority in modern work teams, as softer skills have strong links to well-being and are now an important requirement of team leadership.

Truly effective line managers and team leaders are those who embed coaching into the heart of their management and leadership style (CIPD 2012). In a study of line managers or team leaders and team members within a coaching environment, there was clear confirmation of the existence of a positive relationship between the coaching expertise of the line manager or team leader and team learning outcomes (Bommelje 2015). This observation can represent additional demands on the line manager or team leader when set against the backdrop of recent research, which acknowledged that some managers and leaders find coaching very difficult due to a potential conflict of interest when coaching their own staff (Beattie et al. 2014). Moreover, the innate ability to grow and establish trust with team members takes time and energy from the line manager or team leader which, as established earlier, may be in short supply (Hagen and Aguilar 2012, cited in Beattie et al. 2014). In addition, observers in the field of team leadership have expressed the view that a coach should have relevant experience and a clear methodology, which can place demands on the MAC and coach-like leader (Knights, in EMCC 2018).

Employees are a critical source of competitive advantage (Briner 2012) while recognizing the growing demands and expectations of front-line managers and team leaders in achieving this organizational success. To be successful, the team leader or line manager must demonstrate a willingness to know and understand each team member as a unique individual before trying to help, motivate or develop that person. This implies desire, effort, availability and capability on the part of the line manager or team leader to perform these tasks for each employee in their charge (Briner 2012). This may be considered too high an expectation in some situations. The ability of the line manager or team leader to facilitate a shared vision and values for their team is what will bind them together (Paustain-Underdahl et al. 2013), creating bonds and meaning that will act as a driver for success. The ability to connect fully with team members may be reliant on the line manager or team leader choosing the correct communication modality, which can have a performance impact (Batson and Yoder 2012). All these additional demands and expectations of the line manager or team leader have the potential to create added pressure and can spell success or failure for team functioning.

Effective coaching cannot be sustained over time without the development of mutual trust and a positive regard between the manager or leader and employee (Suriyankietkaew 2013). Feedback within the coaching relationship is an established critical learning tool (Egan and Hamlin 2014), and being data-driven, *possibly from observation or other metrics of assessment*, must be evaluated by the line manager or team leader. This means the evaluation is subject to the line manager or team leader's filter of values, beliefs and experience (Batson and Yoder 2012). This assimilation and evaluation of data and constant self-checking for non-bias and fairness is mentally intensive and demands a high level of self-awareness from the line manager or team leader. Employees may challenge the effectiveness of the MAC or coach-like leader by judging their credibility based on their personal conduct. Feedback at the right time and frequency, in the right manner and when the employee is in a receptive mode can impact the uptake and value of the feedback on the subsequent performance (Peng and Lin 2016). The ability to execute constructive and successful feedback is essential for positive progress and individual development, but may not be a skill all line managers or team leaders possess, even without team dynamics at play. Thus, the ability to offer constructive feedback is a further demand placed on line managers and team leaders.

The debate over whether the MAC or coach-like leader is capable and willing has been documented and is open for discussion. The question arises when asking whether line managers or team leaders *who are expected to execute this coaching style of leadership* want to do so, or are even interested in coaching (Peng and Lin 2016). Other researchers have positioned the issue for the line manager or team leader in terms of lack of time and reward for taking on extra demands, plus having little or no awareness of the need to support subordinates from specific managers and leaders who lack coach-like behaviour

(Beattie et al. 2014). However, on analysis of various approaches to encourage ideas generation, performance improvement and team performance while avoiding conflict within a team, a coaching style does offer an appropriate solution (Paustain-Underdahl et al. 2013).

Consequently, line managers and team leaders are expected to know their team members personally and be cognizant of their unique abilities to recognize individual characteristics to assist in their personal and team development. Further, they need to utilize this enhanced relationship in the early stages of team development to mitigate dysfunctional behaviour developing within the team. In support of this diversionary role away from dysfunctional behaviour, line managers and team leaders do play a critical role in minimizing the attention of team members towards forming any subgroup differences or cliques. They are responsible for shaping the team culture to function as a supportive whole, which is among the most influential activities of any line manager or team leader (Wood et al. 2011), while cultivating the correct individual behaviour for a functioning team and recognizing any signs of dysfunctional behavioural characteristics. These characteristics are an essential requirement for any line manager or team leader intending to initiate peak performance in their team (Kaufmann 2012).

In summary, the role of the line manager or team leader is to build a positive team environment and to foster trust through alignment of team dynamics including culture, team behaviour and functionality (Engelbrecht et al. 2014). The role is reliant on their ability and skill in orchestrating these critical elements for successful team functioning within a constantly changing (Battilana et al. 2010; Clutterbuck 2013) modern business sector (Laud et al. 2016). The demands placed on a MAC or coach-like leader cover a wide perspective and are vast indeed.

Psychological underpinning

In this instance this is not so much a psychology rationale to underpin what the MAC or coach-like leadership style is expected to be in practice, but a specific coaching style that embodies multiple psychological methods (Law 2006).

Coaching is founded on a co-creative narrative approach between the employee and the MAC or coach-like leader. What does this mean? In the coaching world, the coach uses narrative to assist the coachee (or in a team context, the individual team member, or the whole team in the case of team coaching) to achieve their best performance by aligning not only the team's desired outputs and organizational aspirations but their individual goals too. The MAC or coach-like leader would be expected to have developmental conversations with the team members to facilitate and achieve this motivated and aligned state. Therefore, a specific type of narrative is required to achieve this outcome: a co-created approach to establish attachment to the required task by making its achievement paramount to the success of the team and the organization. This meaning-making is not possible without the MAC or coach-like leader knowing their team members and facilitating this through meaningful narrative.

Such narrative in coaching could include metaphors, storytelling, illustrations, timeline visualization and role play to enact a certain outcome – all of which can fully engage the emotions and understanding of the individual. The language used by the MAC or coach-like leader would be relevant to the team context and therefore resonate with each team member. The occurrence of this narrative would likely be at work and therefore offer the opportunity for co-creation of the goals and solutions under discussion. Such application of a narrative provides an active learning opportunity through coaching-styled questions and reflection (after Kolb 1984). These questions would elicit a description of how the individual team member perceives issues and allow added insight for the MAC or coach-like leader to identify areas where alignment is required or avert a potential issue.

Such open and transparent dialogue can provide a collective learning opportunity for team members provided the MAC or coach-like leader can facilitate such an interaction and alignment by reinforcing the collective and personal goals in line with clarification of roles and responsibilities.

Using an appropriate narrative can be powerful and facilitate faster learning through enhanced comprehension. In a fast-paced environment what line manager or team leader would not want to tap into this?

Case study

One day when a team meeting was being held, one of the team members challenged the team leader openly in front of the whole team. The challenge was unjustified and unfounded, but the team leader appreciated the root of the outburst and decided to address it offline. The last thing that was needed was a showdown in front of all the team members. A firm but calm response was delivered.

An understanding of the scenario was that the outburst and challenge came from a senior team member who thought they knew better than their newly appointed team leader. He was flexing his muscles publicly and hoping to gain some points with the other team members. The team leader addressed the challenge openly, stating that they would meet and address this in a more suitable forum, thus communicating to the whole team that there is a time and place for such discussions and being very aware of the importance of the correct environment for constructive feedback. The team leader reserved a hotel room (a neutral and conducive environment to be relaxed and discuss feedback) and met with the individual within 48 hours. The time span was intentional, so as not to allow time for issues to fester too long and to deal with the situation while still fresh in the mind for both, yet giving enough time to engender a more considered and reflected viewpoint. While the individual was not happy at being called into a 1:1 meeting, the team leader used probing questions to elicit the reason why the behaviour of the senior team member had not been considered acceptable. It was important the senior member appreciated and accepted this course of action for progress to be made. In reality, the individual did accept their behaviour was not supportive and did not set a good example for less mature team colleagues.

Since this individual team member thought they were superior in some respect or had insights no one else in the team had, the team leader used the situation to assign to them specific responsibilities and goals, including responsibility for coordinating activities for some of the less experienced team members.

Regular check-ins took place to ensure the senior team member delivered on their assigned responsibilities, which helped prevent a lapse back into previous behavioural patterns and communicate the supportive stance the team leader wanted to exemplify and instil throughout the team. Using this time to understand the team member(s) better also enabled the team leader to apply AMO (Ability, Motivation, Opportunity) – i.e. to better understand their abilities, motivate them by recognizing the supportive aspects within the team and identify opportunities for growth.

The senior team member became very supportive despite requiring regular calibration meetings to support the desired behaviour. In time, the team leader channelled their energy in a more team-supportive manner. Utilizing the invaluable experience of the senior member provided much valued support for less experienced colleagues and improved the functioning of the team. The individual concerned also felt more recognized and satisfied with their role in the team. Thus a solution to meet all needs was possible with meaningful conversation.

Reflective questions

- To what extent do I encourage individual or team reflection or feedback? To what extent do I reward it with praise or other visible or public positive encouragement? What about members of the team; to what extent do I see reflection, feedback or learning being shared? How might this current level be influencing the team climate or environment?

- What evidence do I have about how effective reflection, feedback or learning is for individuals and teams in my organization? How useful was the last set of feedback I received? What about the last set of feedback I offered – to what extent did the situation change after giving the feedback?

- To what extent does my organization encourage reflection, feedback and learning? How is learning embedded so we continually improve? What formal or informal processes do we have, and how are they viewed within and across teams in my organization?

- What mindsets do I hear or see when I am with my team or other team leaders? What do I see as being the effects of those immediately in the context, or subsequently? To what extent do those mindsets let others decide – for themselves – what to do, when, where, why and who with?
- How would I describe my own mindset – if I rerun a previous meeting in my mind, what did I say, how did I say it, what freedoms or instructions did I give? To what extent does my rerun align with my description of my own mindset? What might I like to experiment with next time?
- What behaviours would an ideal manager have in my mind? What about the ideal coach? Where are the overlaps or differences? What does that tell me about what I see as my role? What opportunities or threats are posed by my own approach to leading, managing or coaching?
- How much of what I currently do might be called coaching? When do I find myself not using a coaching approach? What tends to happen in these scenarios? What does that tell me about how I see certain tasks or pressures in certain contexts? What am I risking if I used a coaching approach in these situations?

References

Agarwal, R., Angst, C.M. and Magni, M. (2009). The performance effects of coaching: a multilevel analysis using hierarchical linear modelling, *International Journal of Human Resource Management*, 20(10): 2110–34. DOI: 10.1080/09585190903178054.

Al-Nasser, A. and Mohamed, B. (2015). Examining the relationship between organizational coaching and workplace counterproductive behaviours in the United Arab Emirates, *International Journal of Organizational Analysis*, 23(3): 378–403. DOI: 10.1108/IJOA-08-2014-0793.

Anderson, V. (2013). A Trojan horse? The implications of managerial coaching for leadership theory, *Human Resource Development International*, 1(16): 251–66. DOI: 10.1080/13678868.2013.771868.

Appelbaum, E., Bailey, T., Berg, P. and Kalleberg, A. (2000). *Manufacturing Advantage: Why High-Performance Work Systems Pay Off*. New York: Cornell University Press.

Aquila, A.J. (2007). Dealing with underperforming or dysfunctional partners, *CPA Practice Management Forum* [online], June 3(6).

Bandura, A. (2012). On the functional properties of perceived self-efficacy revisited, *Journal of Management*, 38(1): 9–44. DOI: 10.1177/0149206311410606.

Batson, V.D. and Yoder, L.H. (2012). Managerial coaching: a concept analysis, *Journal of Advanced Nursing*, 68(7.6): 1658–69. doi: 10.1111/j.1365-2648.2011.05840.x.

Battilana, J., Gilmartin, M., Sengul, M., Pache, A.C. and Alexander, J.A. (2010). Leadership competencies for implementing planned organisational change, *Leadership Quarterly*, 21(3): 422–38. DOI:10.1016/j.leaqua.2010.03.007.

Beattie, R.S., Kim, S., Hagen, M.S., Egan, T.M., Ellinger, A.D. and Hamlin, R.G. (2014). Managerial coaching: a review of the empirical literature and development of a model to guide future practice, *Advances in Developing Human Resources*, 16(2): 184–201. DOI:10.1177/1523422313520476.

Belschak, F.D. and Den Hartog, D.N. (2010). Pro-self, pro-social, and pro-organizational foci of proactive behaviour: differential antecedents and consequences, *Journal of Occupational and Organizational Psychology*, 83(2): 475–98.

Berg, M.E. and Karlsen, J.T. (2013). Managing stress in projects using coaching leadership tools, *Engineering Management Journal*, 25(4): 52–61. DOI:10.1080/10429247.2 013.11431995.

Bommelje, R. (2015). Managerial coaching, *New Directions for Adult and Continuing Education* [special issue: *Transforming Adults Through Coaching*], 2015(148): 69–77. https://doi.org/10.1002/ace.20153.

Braun, S., Peus, C., Weisweiler, S. and Frey, D. (2013). Transformational leadership, job satisfaction, and team performance: a multilevel mediation model of trust, *Leadership Quarterly*, 24(1): 270–283. https://doi.org/10.1016/j.leaqua.2012.11.006.

Briner, R.B. (2012). Does coaching work and does anyone really care?, *OP Matters*, 17: 4–12.

Buljac-Samardžić, M. (2012). *Health Teams: Analyzing and Improving Team Performance in Long-Term Care*. Rotterdam: Erasmus University Rotterdam.

Cheng, C., Chua, R.Y.J., Morris, M.W. and Lee, L. (2012). Finding the right mix: how the composition of self-managing multicultural teams' cultural value orientation influences performance over time, *Journal of Organizational Behavior*, 33(3): 389–411.

CIPD (Chartered Institute of Personnel and Development) (2012). *Learning and Talent Development: Annual Survey Report 2012*. London: CIPD. Available at: http://www. digitalopinion.co.uk/files/documents/CIPD_2012_LTD_Report.pdf (accessed 23 January 2023).

Ciporen, R. (2015). The emerging field of executive and organizational coaching: an overview, *New Directions for Adult and Continuing Education*, 2015(148): 5–15.

Clutterbuck, D. (2013). Time to focus coaching on the team, *Industrial and Commercial Training*, 45(1): 18–22.

Cox, E., Bachkirova, T. and Clutterbuck, D. (2014). *The Complete Handbook of Coaching*. London: Sage.

Dahling, J.J., Taylor, S.R., Chau, S.L. and Dwight, S.A. (2016). Does coaching matter? a multilevel model linking managerial coaching skill and frequency to sales goal attainment, *Personnel Psychology*, 69(4): 863–94. DOI: 10.1111/peps.12123.

de Haan, E., Duckworth, A., Birch, D. and Jones, C. (2013). Executive coaching outcome research: the contribution of common factors such as relationship, personality match, and self-efficacy, *Consulting Psychology Journal: Practice and Research*, 65(1): 40–57. DOI:10.1037/a0031635.

Dello Russo, S., Miraglia, M. and Borgogni, A. (2016). Reducing organizational politics in performance appraisals: the role of coaching leaders for age-diverse employees: OPPA and coaching leadership, *Human Resource Management*, 56(5): 769–83.

Driskell, T., Salas, E. and Driskell, J.E. (2017). Teams in extreme environments: alterations in team development and teamwork, *Human Resource Management Review*, 28(4): 434–49. http://dx.doi.org/10.1016/j.hrmr.2017.01.002.

Egan, T. and Hamlin, R.G. (2014). Coaching, HRD, and relational richness: putting the pieces together, *Advances in Developing Human Resources*, 16(2): 242–57.

Ehrhardt, K., Miller, J.S., Freeman, S.J. and Hom, P.W. (2013). Examining project commitment in cross-functional teams: antecedents and relationship with team performance, *Journal of Business and Psychology*, 29(3): 443–61. DOI: 10.1007/s10869-013-9325.

Ellinger, A.D. (2013). Supportive supervisors and managerial coaching: exploring their intersections, *Journal of Occupational and Organizational Psychology*, 86(3): 310–16.

Ellinger, A.D., Beattie, R.S., Hamlin, R.G., Wang, Y. and Trolan, O. (2006). The manager as coach: a review of empirical literature and the development of a tentative model of managerial coaching, in F. Poell (ed.) *Proceedings of the Seventh International Conference on HRD Research and Practice across Europe*. Tilburg: University of Tilburg.

Engelbrecht, A.S., Heine, G. and Mahembe, B. (2014). The influence of ethical leadership on trust and work engagement: an exploratory study, *SA Journal of Industrial Psychology*, 40(1): article 2010. https://doi.org/10.4102/sajip.v40i1.1210.

EMCC (European Mentoring and Coaching Council) (2018). *Coaching and Ethics in Practice: Dilemmas, Navigations, and the (Un)spoken*, Research Policy and Practice Provocation Series. Poole: EMCC.

Ewen, C., Wihler, A., Blickle, G. et al. (2013). Further specification of the leader political skill – leadership effectiveness relationships: transformational and transactional leader behavior as mediators, *Leadership Quarterly*, 24(4): 516–33.

Fairhurst, G. and Connaughton, S.L. (2014). Leadership: a communication perspective, *Leadership*, 10(1): 7–35. DOI: 10.1177/1742715013509396.

Fleishman, E.A. (1992). Taxonomic efforts in the description of leader behavior: a synthesis and functional interpretation, *Leadership Quarterly*, 2(4): 245–87.

Gerard, L., McMillan, J. and D'Annunzio-Green, N. (2017). Conceptualising sustainable leadership, *Industrial and Commercial Training*, 49(3): 116–26.

Hackman, J.R. (2002). *Leading Teams: Setting the Stage for Great Performance*. Boston, MA: Harvard Business School Press.

Hagen, M.S. and Peterson, S.L. (2013). Measuring coaching: behavioural and skill-based managerial coaching, *Journal of Management Development*, 34(2): 114–33.

Hall, J.L. (2013). Managing teams with diverse compositions: implications for managers from research on the faultline model, *Advanced Management Journal*, 78(1): 4–10.

Hur, Y., van den Berg, P.T. and Wilderon, C.P.M. (2011). Transformational leadership as a mediator between emotional intelligence and team outcomes, *Leadership Quarterly*, 22(4): 591–603.

Jones, R., Woods, S. and Guillaume, Y. (2016). The effectiveness of workplace coaching: a meta-analysis of learning and performance outcomes from coaching, *Journal of Occupational and Organizational Psychology*, 89(2): 249–77. DOI:10.1111/joop.12119.

Karaçivi, A. and Demirel, A. (2014). A futuristic commentary: coach-like leadership, *International Journal of Business and Social Science*, 5(9): 126–33.

Katzenbach, J.R. and Smith, D.K. (1999). *The Wisdom of Teams: Creating the High-Performance Organization*. London: Harper Business.

Kaufmann, B. (2012). The anatomy of dysfunctional working relationships, *Business Strategy Series*, 13(2): 102–6.

Keyton, J. (1999). Analyzing interaction patterns in dysfunctional teams, *Small Group Research*, 30(4): 491–518.

Kiefer, T. and Barclay, L.J. (2012). Understanding the mediating role of toxic emotional experiences in the relationship between negative emotions and adverse outcomes, *Journal of Occupational and Organizational Psychology*, 85(4): 600–25.

Kim, S. (2014). Assessing the influence of managerial coaching on employee outcomes, *Human Resource Development Quarterly*, 25(1): 59–85.

Kim, S., Egan, T.M., Kim, W. and Kim, J. (2013). The impact of managerial coaching behavior on employee work-related reactions, *Journal of Business and Psychology*, 28(3): 315–30.

Kivipõld, K. (2015). Organizational leadership capability – a mechanism of knowledge coordination for inducing innovative behaviour. A case study in Estonian service industries, *Baltic Journal of Management*, 10(4): 478–96. DOI: 10.1108/BJM-10-2014-0152.

Kollée, J.A., Giessner, J.M., Steffen, R. and van Knippenberg, D. (2013). Leader evaluations after performance feedback: the role of follower mood, *Leadership Quarterly*, 24(1): 203–14.

Laud, R., Arevalo, J. and Johnson, M. (2016). The changing nature of managerial skills, mindsets and roles: advancing theory and relevancy for contemporary managers, *Journal of Management & Organization*, 22(4): 435–56.

Lin, W. (2015). Leading future orientations for current effectiveness: the role of engagement and supervisor coaching in linking future work self-salience to job performance, *Journal of Vocational Behavior*, 92: 145–56.

London, M. and Mone, E.M. (2015). Designing feedback to achieve performance improvement, in K. Kraiger, J. Passmore, S. Malvezzi and N. Rebelo dos Santos (eds) *The Wiley Blackwell Handbook of the Psychology of Training, Development, and Performance Improvement*. Chichester, West Sussex: Wiley Blackwell, pp. 462–85.

Nansubuga, F., Munene, J.C. and Ntayi, J.M. (2015). Can reflection boost competences development in organisations?, *European Journal of Training and Development*, 39(6): 504–21. http://dx.doi.org/10.1108/EJTD-01-2015-0004.

O'Broin, A. and McDowall, A. (2015). Specificity is the key, if we really want to understand coaching!, *Coaching: An International Journal of Theory, Research and Practice*, 8(6): 69–72.

Passmore, J.A. (2010). A grounded theory study of the coachee experience: the implications for training and practice in coaching psychology, *International Coaching Psychology Review*, 5(1): 48–62.

Paustain-Underdahl, S.C., Shanock, L.R. and Rogelberg, S.G. (2013). Antecedents to supportive supervision: an examination of biographical data, *Journal of Occupational and Organizational Psychology*, 86(3): 288–309.

Peng, J.C. and Lin, J. (2016). Linking supervisor feedback environment to contextual performances: the mediating effect of leader–member exchange, *Leadership & Organization Development Journal*, 37(6): 802–20.

Pousa, C. and Mathieu, A. (2015). The influence of coaching on employee performance: results from two international quantitative studies, *Performance Improvement Quarterly*, 27(3): 75–92.

Pulakos, E.D., Mueller-Hanson, R.A., O'Leary, R.S. and Meyrowitz, M.M. (2012). *Building a High-Performance Culture: A Fresh Look at Performance Management*, SHRM Foundation Effective Practice Guidelines Series. Alexandria, VA: SHRM Foundation.

Schippers, M.C., Homan, A.C. and Knippenberg, D.V. (2013). To reflect or not to reflect: prior team performance as a boundary condition of the effects of reflexivity on learning and final team performance, *Journal of Organizational Behavior*, 34(1): 6–23. DOI:10.1002/job.1784.

Suriyankietkaew, K. (2013). Emergent leadership paradigms for corporate sustainability: a proposed model, *Journal of Applied Business Research*, 29(1): 173–82.

Tocan, M.C. and Chindris-Vasioiu, O. (2013). Modern organizations and the challenges of the new century, *Knowledge Horizons – Economics*, 5(3): 57–60.

Vincent-Hoper, S., Muser, C. and Janneck, M. (2012). Transformational leadership, work engagement and occupational success, *Career Development International*, 17(7): 663–82.

Wakkee, I., Elfring, T. and Monagham, S. (2010). Creating entrepreneurial employees in traditional service sectors: the role of coaching and self-efficacy, *International Entrepreneurship and Management Journal*, 6(1): 1–121.

Wood, S., Michaelides, G. and Thomson, C. (2011). Team approach, idea generation, conflict and performance, *Team Performance Management: An International Journal*, 17(7/8): 382–404. http://dx.doi.org/10.1108/13527591111182643.
Zoltan, R. (2015). Group dynamics and team functioning in an organisational context, *Ecoforum*, 4(2): 154–8.

Psychological references

Kolb, D.A. (1984). *Experiential Learning: Experience as a Source of Learning and Development*. Englewood Cliffs, NJ: Prentice Hall.
Law, H.C. (2006). Can coaches be good in any context?, *Coaching at Work*, 1(2): 14.

8 Insights and recommendations

Summary

This chapter reviews the insights and recommendations drawn from the 30 interviews of line managers and team leaders who employ coaching as their modus operandi, and shares multiple examples and quotations to illustrate and augment the team effectiveness models as previously referenced.

Keywords: team challenge, establishing trust, safe environment, clarity of direction, coaching interpersonal focus and benefits

Introduction

Some of the literature previously reviewed has provided pivotal insights into the complexity of teams. Several authors (including Engelbrecht et al. 2014) agree that teams are dynamic, making many of the elements of managing a team even more challenging for the line manager or team leader, whose key responsibility is to facilitate effective team functioning (Battilana et al. 2010; Clutterbuck 2013; Fairhurst and Connaughton 2014; Laud et al. 2016). The established team effectiveness models (see Table 3.1) have indicated many of the essential elements to facilitate a functioning team, including mention of coaching as part of the solution. The specific role coaching plays in achieving a functioning team when employed by a line manager or team leader has yet to be fully explored, which is the foundation and driver for the research culminating in this book. The literature highlights the increasing demands being placed on line managers leading to the evolution of MAC and coach-like leader as a potential solution for addressing team challenge (Anderson 2013; Dahling et al. 2016). Combining Table 3.1 (Team effectiveness models) with the summary behaviours from Table 5.1 (Comparison of unproductive or dysfunctional behaviours) provides the visual boundaries and conceptual framework for exploration into how the MAC or coach-like leader may deliver a functioning team and mitigate dysfunctional behaviour (see Figure 8.1).

Figure 8.1 Conceptual framework

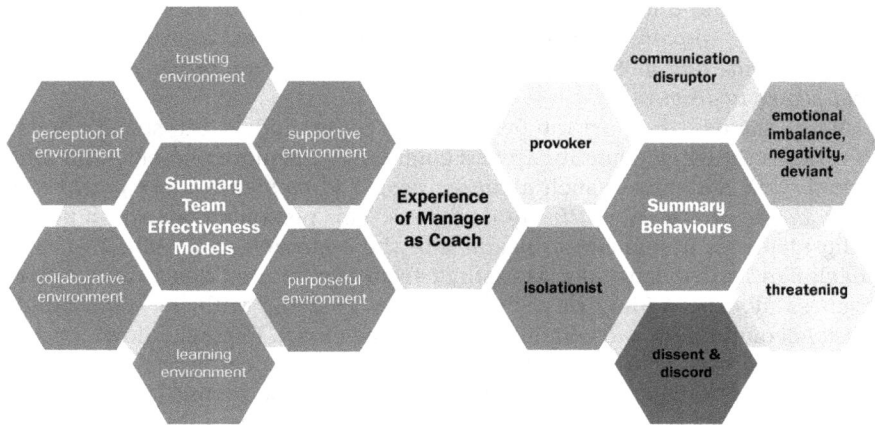

Aims

This chapter aims to consolidate the findings and effectiveness insights from Chapter 7 leading to the development of templates, models and self-assessment that a MAC or coach-like leader may apply within their workplace. There is also an explanation of the potential application of these tools and how they may be adapted and tailored for your team and organization.

Dealing with team challenge

We will explore the advice from the 30 line managers and team leaders interviewed to seek guidance in addressing each of these challenges.

Establishing trust, accountability and commitment

The issue of how enabling structures (see the team effectiveness models) support the prevention of unproductive or dysfunctional behaviour is viewed through the perspective of the interview data, as follows:

> *Without trust, it is not going to happen and that is the second most important item, whereas equal first most important thing I would say for me is having the structure and having the trust.*

There are potential methods to foster accountability and commitment, as indicated by the following statements: *encourage open discussion, an open environment, empower people to step up, place opportunities in front of your staff, motivate and mobilize them, draw them into the narrative of decisions, hold people to account.*

While the data support the team effectiveness models, the specific focus to establish trust, accountability and commitment is more personal and individual, with statements such as *allow people to step into their power* and *draw them into the narrative of decisions.* This personal connection potentially identifies a significant insight into the approach which the MAC and coach-like leader may take as distinct from the broader-based team effectiveness models. Adding this extra layer of enabling with the team builds trust, accountability and commitment from the outset. Further, allowing team members to *step into their power* indicates confidence on the part of the line manager or team leader towards the team member, permitting ownership and accountability for the task in hand. This commitment and appreciation in terms of trust and reliance illustrates the value of *draw(ing) them into the narrative of decisions.*

Creating a safe environment

From the interview data, facilitating a safe environment and reflective space is an important requirement of organizational support:

> With somebody in the same office, you put the kettle on and you have a quick chat over lunch about other things and I suppose that bonding bit happens a lot quicker, whereas I'm getting it to fit in ... quite formal at the beginning and it's only now as we're building up the trust that we're getting to know a little bit more and they're telling me things now that they wouldn't have dreamt of them telling me.

The data documented the need to *create the right environment, create an open environment, establish an open environment, correct environment, create an environment for contribution, create a learning space, create space and environment to coach, avoid degrading, designated space, know the importance of space, space to learn together, reflective space.* One line manager interviewed was responsible for resolving team issues related to health and safety on an oil rig. Space and environment were considered of great importance when captive on an offshore platform:

> The importance of achieving the right environment for coaching or one-to-one conversation to take place, promoting a neutral space on the oil rig was in the cinema for the safe environment to contribute, reflect and learn. The cinema was often referred to as 'our space', which facilitated the correct environment.

Figure 8.2 Importance of space

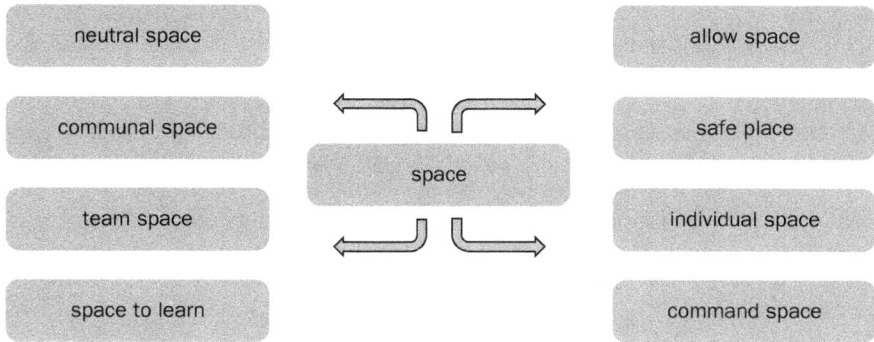

A recognition of the need to feel safe to promote a successful functioning of the team has long been recognized by team effectiveness models, authors and leading authorities from different fields of research, including psychology. For example, Maslow's Hierarchy of Needs (1943) identified safety and the need to feel safe and secure as among the required foundational elements en route towards full actualization and realization of our full potential. The importance of space for addressing unproductive or dysfunctional behaviour while *avoiding degrading* an individual in an open space environment was reported as essential since privacy is often required to make the space safe. The data on space is highlighted in Figure 8.2.

Analysis of interview data relating to the environment and space confers the important need to create a conducive working climate by dealing with specific individual and team challenges. Dexter (2010) lists the essential criteria for team success as people, task, process, location and facilities, reinforcing the role that space and environment play in successful team working. Having a *designated space*, or possibly a neutral space, to conduct coaching or engage in difficult conversations was identified as a requirement to achieve success from the discussion.

Facilitating the right atmosphere through engineering the correct environment, as in *creating space to learn* or *reflect*, strengthens the importance and the need for line managers and team leaders to consider the impact that space or environment may have on the team or the recipient's mindset. It will also affect their ability to absorb and apply the content of the conversation. If this conversation is taking place publicly, the individual is likely to be concerned about their team members being privy to the conversation and being observed during such a discourse. These observations can be linked to the specific element in the team effectiveness model relating to minimizing distractions (Edmondson, cited in Ghosh et al. 2012) where work environment is perceived as *safe*, releasing the worker to focus on the task in hand and improve efficiency and potential performance.

Once more, the advice of the managers interviewed moves towards a more personal approach in the creation of space. Feeling safe is a basic human need, and it will prove detrimental to the team if managers ignore this in the workplace and fail to facilitate a *safe* environment to *contribute, reflect* and *learn*. One of the required pillars of the organizational climate (Al-Nasser and Mohamed 2015) to engender positive work-related attitudes and behaviours is that of certainty, which is a facet of safety. A safe working environment is one where team members feel *safe* to *contribute*, support a *team spirit* and achieve *harmony* among the team members to share in open dialogue and learn from each another. This was a desired aim as relayed from the interview data, and a key enabler in addressing dysfunctional behaviour with clarity of direction.

Clarity of direction

Clarity of direction is represented and identified in the established team effectiveness models (Table 3.1) and supported strongly by the interview data with statements such as *have clear direction, start with a summary of the task or goal* and *be clear about when and how*. One quotation from an interviewee provides such confirmation as:

> *Setting a clear direction, the idea is that the leaders and managers should make sure the direction of the business is clear but also, they have to set a clear direction on a day-by-day basis so everyone understands where they're trying to go and how they should be going there, not in terms of the activity but the type of journey they're going on.*

Clarity and focus, as referenced by the interview data, clearly have a personal focus as indicated in Figure 8.3, with added statements such as *defining roles and tasks, communicating on their level, summarizing* and *providing*

Figure 8.3 Clarity and focus

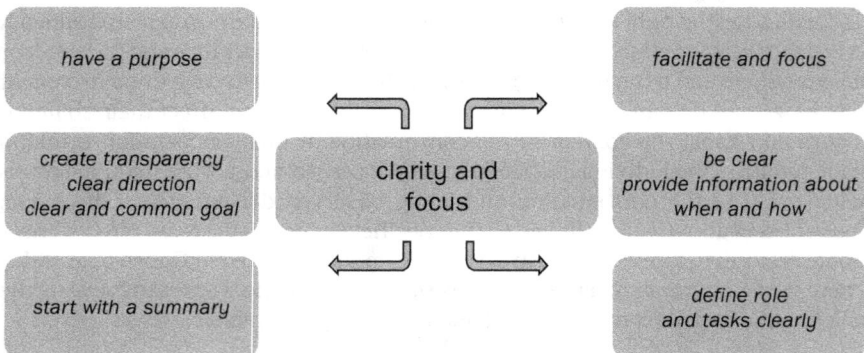

information, which achieve clarity for the individual and team, creating *transparency* of *purpose*.

Researchers in this field, Fairhurst and Connaughton (2014), support communication as a conduit for achieving a desired behaviour, and describe communication as a transmission channel. The communication context leads through dialectics via discussion, reasoning *generating meaning*, and active dialogue *narrative* versus the traditional hierarchical leadership style of *telling*, evolving willing leadership (Conway and Coyle-Shapiro 2012) and engagement with the team members *having a clear direction, focus* and *providing information to the team about when and how*.

Table 8.1 compares Fairhurst and Connaughton's six communication conduits with interview feedback (data) from the managers on means of achieving the desired behaviour.

One important element from Fairhurst and Connaughton, as endorsed by the interview data, relates to language as referenced by the use of *correct language and reflecting back, in their* (team members') *own language*. The data and advice from the managers revealed associated facets such as *using metaphors and stories, framing for understanding*, plus *investing in all forms of communication* and *starting conversations*. This was previously discussed in Chapter 7 during a review of the use of narrative as a means of establishing

Table 8.1 Communication conduits with representative manager feedback (Fairhurst and Connaughton 2014)

Fairhurst & Connaughton (2014) six communication conduits for developing desired behaviour	Representative interview data
being meaning-centred	*be clear about when and how, start with a summary*
being relational with no bias on parties communicating	*create transparency, common goal, non-judgemental*
creating influential acts of organizing	*define roles clearly, know work priorities*
leading with and through dialectics	*have clear direction, robust dialogue, have a coaching conversation, start conversations*
creating diversity and being global	*create transparency, and facilitating focus and communicating on their level*
communication should be alive with the potential to reflect and bring about moral accountability and change	*facilitate, provide information to the team on how and what, be in the moment, reflect and be reflective*

real understanding. The aspect of competence applied by the line managers and team leaders *as interviewed* relates to the potential to exploit advanced forms of communication and language patterns, provided the line manager or team leader knows and understands individual team members. This advanced communication skill, as encompassed within coaching, is explored in the following section.

Coaching: interpersonal focus and benefits

The following quotation was an interviewee's opinion of a line manager as coach or coach-like leader:

> I think you can be trained in anything; I could probably learn Russian if I had to and put my mind to it. But I think people who are in positions of management, and they are competent and they're competent as managers, and when we do coaching skills for managers training internally, I've seen some managers stick all the way through a coaching course and at the end of it saying – now I know what I need to tell my team! And you just think, you haven't quite got the gist of it. So, I think you can be competent, but I think to be good at something, it has to be part of you, and you have to have a passion for it.

Whether there is agreement with this opinion or not, it is true that some line managers and team leaders will find the journey of becoming a MAC or a coach-like leader easier than others. There has been much research and management study in the past on the necessary characteristics of becoming a competent leader and manager. But if a coaching style is adopted, it has to be genuinely driven by a desire to support and for team members to excel. This self-sacrificing type of leadership in favour of supporting our team members is a foundational platform for a fully functioning team. And another interviewee shared:

> Don't restrict their thinking – or they will always expect you to tell them what to do ... Help them change with cognitive restructuring.

Figure 8.4 highlights statements from the line manager data as part of the team effectiveness element relating to coaching, interpersonal focus, problem-solving and enhanced learning. The coaching characteristics relate to some of the skills required to fulfil the role of a coach and be coach-minded. A definition of coaching from the manager data is that *it's about helping an individual or a team through active listening*. The data did reveal listening as an important attribute, as *listen* was referenced seven times, *listening skills* three times, including to *listen and reflect* and *listen to your team* and finally *completely*

Figure 8.4 Coaching attributes

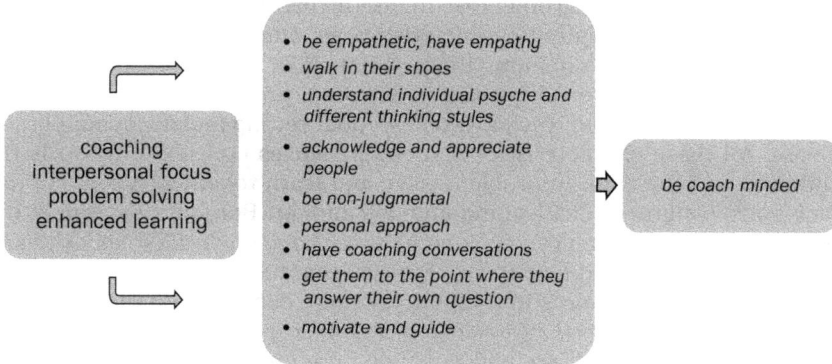

listen. The importance of listening featured prominently among the communication skills listed by the managers as part of *coaching conversations*. Listening is an integral part of the *personal approach*.

Action-focused dialogue develops a change in thinking, behaviour, learning and emotions (Berg and Karlsen 2013) as in *cognitive restructuring*, mentioned by one line manager, which relies on advanced communication skills as in *coaching conversations* for addressing unproductive or dysfunctional behaviour. Coaching is about asking the right questions (Berg and Karlsen 2013). The advice shared by the managers and leaders interviewed included *ask the right questions* in addition to *ask questions, ask good questions, talk to staff*, and *question them, ask what their challenges are*. This advice was broadened to *question for clarity* and to *break down problems, learn as you go*. The latter, *learning as you go*, was as much an aphorism for the line manager and team leader as it was for the team member, thereby enhancing their appreciation of each individual within the team. This ability to question *to get them* [team members] *to the point of answering their own issues* is an essential skill of the MAC and coach-like leader, plus a crucial requirement to bring about change (*cognitive restructuring*) and a harmonious team climate.

The focus of questioning from the line manager and team leader perspective was to *gain understanding*, which allowed *reasoning* with the team member and promoting awareness. Understanding was viewed as a basic tenet for the MAC or coach-like leader in correctly addressing team challenge. Phrases like *understand the drama behind the behaviour, understand characteristics and know when to step in, intervene with the appropriate solution when you understand* endorse an observation from experts that a coach must possess effective communication skills, be a good observer, an excellent listener and know how and when to provide feedback (Berg and Karlsen 2013). This approach from the line manager and team leader interviews is aligned with a coaching style proposed by other researchers in this area, Karavici and Demirel (2014), who list the required characteristics as: emotional intelligence, self-awareness, self-regulation, motivation, social skills and empathy, coach-like leadership, asking powerful questions, listening, providing direct communication feedback, creating trust, awareness, goal setting and accountability of process. All these characteristics and competencies contribute towards the requirement of the team to problem-solve and learn together. Achieving this coaching role status is challenging and demanding (Berg and Karlsen 2013), and explains data references such as *be tenacious, don't allow emotions to derail, be impartial* and *be passive*. Further characteristics expected of line managers and team leaders in a highly dynamic context with multiple team players relate to *transmit information* and *gain perspectives*, while at the same time *achieving balance* and maintaining an individual focus. *Creating opportunities for staff* among other demands may seem impossible, but if effective collaboration and teamwork are to be achieved the line manager or team leader must *enable and develop people* by *connecting their individual ambitions* with the *opportunities* within the team, *capitalizing on team intelligence* to solve problems and enhance team learning in synchronicity. To achieve this range of competence requires a level of collaborative teamwork, as discussed below.

Collaborative team working

The following quotation from one of the interviewed line managers and team leaders captures the essence and importance of teamwork in the team effectiveness models (see Table 3.1): that organizations rely increasingly on teamwork and collaboration:

> *This requires the commitment of those involved to give themselves the space to be together and learn together and a belief that whatever time they spend together will pay for itself many times over in performance once they have achieved a level of teamwork that only that kind of space can generate.*

Other observers, such as Karlgaard (2013), have declared that collaborative team members can work smarter and faster through sharing tacit and implicit knowledge and leveraging knowledge-sharing which exists simultaneously at the individual, collective or organizational level (Kivipõld 2015). Collaboration has many advantages (Figure 8.5) aside from being able to work smarter and faster, but it is reliant on the MAC or coach-like leader facilitating this facet correctly to reap its full benefits within the team.

The actions by the MAC or coach-like leader to facilitate collaboration also impact the perception of the individual team members, as explored below.

Figure 8.5 Collaborative benefits of teamwork

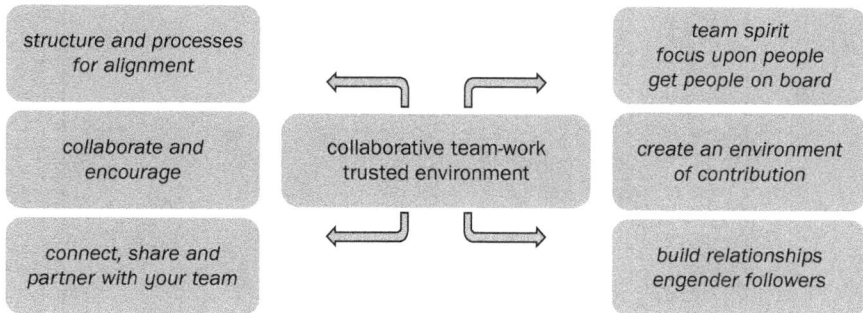

structure and processes for alignment		team spirit focus upon people get people on board
collaborate and encourage	collaborative team-work trusted environment	create an environment of contribution
connect, share and partner with your team		build relationships engender followers

Perceived outcomes and improved learning capabilities

The following statement supports an established team role accepting that the MAC or coach-like leader ventures into individual-based aspects of team effectiveness in support of a more personal appreciation of team members' individual skills and the promotion of self-expression.

> I had a team in a local newspaper and the newspaper was on its last legs and was going to be closed, and I brought the group together to get them to better understand each other and the values that they were bringing and the qualities that they had and asked them to work differently as a result of the need to rescue the paper but also to express themselves. And that newspaper was not only saved but two years later won a national award for being the best written newspaper.

This example from a MAC or coach-like leader utilizes many of the elements referenced earlier such as trust, empowerment, collective focus and inclusion of team members in the challenge and formulation of the goals to be addressed.

There are issues which have not been addressed in the team effectiveness models (Table 3.1) which relate to specific behavioural changes of individuals in our teams, and particularly those that can lead to conflict. Table 8.2 illustrates the behaviours that are addressed by the team effectiveness models (left-hand side), but when the challenging behaviours that are commonplace in teams are reviewed (right-hand side), it can be appreciated how a MAC or coach-like leader can support and create an enhanced, conducive environment to address unproductive and dysfunctional behaviour in a time-efficient manner. In the pace of change in our modern teams, managers need to address these issues *with haste* for a team to function at full potential.

The benefit to being coach-minded is reviewed in Chapter 9.

Table 8.2 Behavioural issues – team effectiveness models

Summary team effectiveness models	Behaviour issues addressed by team effectiveness models	Behaviour issues not addressed by team effectiveness models	No. of supportive interviewees
trust, accountability & commitment as enabling structures	discord, seek a scapegoat (Keyton) does not trust colleagues, does not communicate well, fails to follow up, works too few hours to produce desired output (Aquila) not trusting, dissent (Kaufmann) disconnected, not engaged (Kiefer) absence of shared responsibility (Kaufmann)	never their fault (Aquila) primary provoker in disruption (Keyton) lacks emotional intelligence (Aquila) hoards work, unwilling to delegate (Aquila)	**16**
organizational support create a safe environment	increases stress for whole team (Keyton) increased risk, increased operational issues (Kaufmann) reduces energy, diminished psychological health (Kiefer)	conflict allowed to spiral (Kaufmann) false threats (Aquila) emotions unregulated (Kiefer)	**13**
clarity of direction meaningful purpose minimize distractions focus on goals	unable lo deliver (Aquila) interactions create confusion, confuse situation (Keyton) increased implementation problems (Kaufmann) attention away from task (Kiefer)	toxic to whole team (Kiefer) does not participate in team events (Aquila) insecure (Aquila)	**18**

Table 8.2 *(Continued)*

Summary team effectiveness models	Behaviour issues addressed by team effectiveness models	Behaviour issues not addressed by team effectiveness models	No. of supportive interviewees
coaching interpersonal focus problem-solving enhanced learning	wants to be centre of attention, negative attitude, deviant behaviour, problematic (Keyton) abnormal or impaired behaviour, sub-optimal performer, prone to disagreements, lack-lustre decision-making, passive-aggressive, prone to quarrelling (Kaufmann) becomes overly aggressive (Aquila)	draining for whole team (Kiefer) creates attentional demands (Kiefer) polar opposite of functional (Kaufmann)	7
collaborative teamwork trusted environment	lets the team down (Aquila) drives away, isolates (Aquila) prevents team being effective, ineffective, frustrating (Kaufmann) things can only be done their way (Aquila) displaces others (Keyton)	not a team player (Aquila) manipulative (Aquila) unrealistic promises (Aquila) often accepts wrong type of work (Aquila)	14
perceived outcomes improved learning and capabilities	plants doubts (Keyton) difference of opinion (Kaufmann)	unable to sustain the role in isolation (Keyton)	18

Psychological underpinning

In this section we start from the perspective of a MAC or leader adopting a coach-like style or working with a new team or team member. In this scenario there is considerable learning required from both sides to establish the rapport and trust as referenced earlier as essential for an effective coaching relationship. Starting with a focus in mind, an intent and a desired outcome for each team member to be successful, our aim would be for team members to reach their desired destination without having to instruct them.

Starting as we mean to go on regarding empowering team members and creating opportunities for their growth as a MAC or coach-like leader, we would wish to assess the competency of each team member. This would be achieved using a co-constructive approach to build engagement and ownership of the individuals and their team tasks – by creating a consensus and allowing each team member to approach the task according to their chosen route and gain ownership for a distinct task as part of the whole. Not wishing to disappoint fellow team members will be part of the driver at play by allowing them to prove their competency and capabilities to each other as well as to the line manager or team leader in achieving required outcomes.

This style of co-creation has evolved to become what some coaches refer to as *solutions-focused coaching*. This is an effective approach in focusing on the final achievement rather than the problem or task in hand (which sometimes can block our view of possibilities) or the manner in which we get there. This really does create focus and (for some) motivation, as well as building on existing skills the team members already possess, thereby identifying areas for potential development. To avoid failure, we need to match the task to the person where possible, but we can allow free rein with a few simple questions to ensure the team member understands the expectation placed upon them, achieved through a clarifying coaching-based conversation.

A solutions-focused approach allows team members to try different things, be creative, collaborate or work solo since the focus is set on achieving the task in hand. *The successful solution is the focus.* When one solution does not work, then trying another solution builds skills and knowledge. As a MAC or coach-like leader, we need to facilitate and allow these opportunities to take place.

Self-directed learning is suggested as a platform for such activities. A solutions-focused model has been created by Williams, Palmer and O'Connell (2011) with the stages presented in the following case study.

S – share updates
O – observe interest
L – listen to goals
U – understand exceptions (or expectations)
T – tap into potential within the team
I – imagine success – as a motivator
O – own the outcome
N – note contribution – this will inform team working and collaborations

Case study

Where there are arguments between team members the solutions-focused model outlined above can help to support the MAC or coach-like leader to achieve the outcome they desire for the benefit of the whole team.

S – share updates – this should be facilitated by the manager or leader to allow mutual understanding of one another

O – observe interest – who is engaging, who isn't, so you know who to have a one-to-one with

L – listen – active listening to really appreciate what is being said

U – understand exceptions (or expectations) – *understand* was a key factor supported by the 30 managers interviewed for this book research

T – tap into potential within the team – know who you can buddy up with weaker team members, who can have a positive influence, who can share their competencies

I – imagine success – as a motivator, share this frequently and bring it alive for team members to keep focused on it

O – own the outcome – as a team and individuals – what has been their pivotal contribution – recognize that, praise where possible, don't leave anyone out – inspire

N – note contribution – this will inform team working and collaborations. This is also about celebrating contributions from each team member and as a whole team. If they achieved the task or goal set then that is worth a 'shout out'. Recognition doesn't cost us anything but can be so inspiring.

When this model is applied in practice, any arguments that may have been ongoing should pale into the background with the focus being reset on the task.

Reflective questions

- What am I doing to establish trust in my teams? How do I balance that with accountability in a safe environment? What am I doing to establish direction, and commitment to that direction, in the teams? How am I balancing that with spaces for positive feedback and learning?
- What processes do I have for sharing updates? How do I know this is reaching the team and that they understand what I am intending to communicate?
- To what extent do I observe interest to know who is engaging, who is not, and those who you do not know about?
- How often do I listen actively so I appreciate what is being stated? How often do I understand exceptions or expectations?
- What is my approach to know and then tap into potential within my teams? What do I do to enable peer sharing and learning so the whole team grows as a result?

- To what extent, and how often, do I show my vision for success? When was the last time I shared this, and how vivid was my vision for others? How do I know?
- To what extent do I own the outcomes of the team? To what extent does the team as a whole own the outcomes? How often do I reward or praise the team when the team, or individuals within it, own the outcomes?
- How often are contributions and achievements celebrated visibly for the team? How do the team or individuals within it receive the celebrations?

References

Al-Nasser, A. and Mohamed, B. (2015). Examining the relationship between organizational coaching and workplace counterproductive behaviours in the United Arab Emirates, *International Journal of Organizational Analysis*, 23(3): 378–403. DOI: 10.1108/IJOA-08-2014-0793.

Anderson, V. (2013). A Trojan horse? The implications of managerial coaching for leadership theory, *Human Resource Development International*, 1(16): 251–66. DOI:10.1080/13678868.2013.771868.

Battilana, J., Gilmartin, M., Sengul, M., Pache, A.C. and Alexander, J.A. (2010). Leadership competencies for implementing planned organisational change, *Leadership Quarterly*, 21(3): 422–38. DOI:10.1016/j.leaqua.2010.03.007.

Berg, M.E. and Karlsen, J.T. (2013). Managing stress in projects using coaching leadership tools, *Engineering Management Journal*, 25(4): 52–61. DOI: 10.1080/10429247. 2013.11431995.

Clutterbuck, D. (2013). Time to focus coaching on the team, *Industrial and Commercial Training*, 45(1): 18–22.

Conway, N. and Coyle-Shapiro, J.A.M. (2012). The reciprocal relationship between psychological contract fulfilment and employee performance and the moderating role of perceived organisational support and tenure, *Journal of Occupational and Organizational Psychology*, 85(2): 277–99.

Dahling, J.J. , Taylor, S.R., Chau, S.L. and Dwight, S.A. (2016). Does coaching matter? a multilevel model linking managerial coaching skill and frequency to sales goal attainment, *Personnel Psychology*, 69(4): 863–94. DOI: 10.1111/peps.12123.

Dexter, B. (2010). Critical success factors for developmental team projects, *Team Performance Management: An International Journal*, 16(7/8): 343–58. http://dx.doi.org/ 10.1108/13527591011090637.

Engelbrecht, A.S., Heine, G. and Mahembe, B. (2014). The influence of ethical leadership on trust and work engagement: an exploratory study, *SA Journal of Industrial Psychology*, 40(1): article 2010. https://doi.org/10.4102/sajip.v40i1.1210.

Fairhurst, G. and Connaughton, S.L. (2014). Leadership: a communication perspective, *Leadership*, 10(1): 7–35. DOI: 10.1177/1742715013509396.

Ghosh, R., Shuck, B. and Petrosko, J. (2012). Emotional intelligence and organisational learning in work teams, *Journal of Management Development*, 31(6): 603–19.

Karaçivi, A. and Demirel, A. (2014). A futuristic commentary: coach-like leadership, *International Journal of Business and Social Science*, 5(9): 126–33.

Karlgaard, R. (2013). Team management: think small and agile. Forbes website, 13 November. Available at: http://www.forbes.com/sites/richkarlgaard/2013/11/13/team-management-think-small-and-agile/ (accessed 13 January 2023).

Kivipõld, K. (2015). Organizational leadership capability – a mechanism of knowledge coordination for inducing innovative behaviour. A case study in Estonian service industries, *Baltic Journal of Management*, 10(4): 478–96. DOI: 10.1108/BJM-10-2014-0152.

Laud, R., Arevalo, J. and Johnson, M. (2016). The changing nature of managerial skills, mindsets and roles: advancing theory and relevancy for contemporary managers, *Journal of Management & Organization*, 22(4): 435–56.

Psychology reference

Williams, H., Palmer, S. and O'Connell, B. (2011). Introducing SOLUTIONS and FOCUS: two solution-focused models, *Coaching Psychology International*, 4(1): 6–9.

9 MAC: development of templates

Summary

This chapter consolidates the findings and effectiveness insights leading to the development of templates, models and self-assessments as informed by the line manager and team leader interviews. It gives an explanation of the potential application of these tools and how they may be adapted and tailored to your team, organization and overall purpose.

Keywords: being coach-minded, time to act, coaching conduct

Introduction

The addition of established templates with the knowledge, observation and findings from the interview data offers an enlightened and modern data approach to leading and managing teams. The creation of these templates and self-assessments is intended to assist with self-reflection and judgement relating to your ability to adopt a coaching style of leading and managing your team. If there is a willingness to strive towards embracing this coaching style of leadership and management, you can rest assured that you will reap the many benefits for yourself, your team members and your organization. We hope you will consider and review the tools provided and take ownership of them to encompass them within your context and with your team members.

It would be a delight to hear from you and receive your feedback with comments and to learn from your experience of the application of insights in your practice and adoption of a coaching style of management and leadership.

Aims

The aim of this chapter is to share resources and tools to facilitate the paradigm shift in leadership and management as discussed in this book. By reading and absorbing the reflective exercises and opportunities, you will have learned a great deal about matching your ability with the required competency to encompass a coaching style of management and leadership. Therefore we are offering an AMO scenario to you here and now. We recognize that if you have got to this stage in the book, you are likely to have given these tools a fair assessment to enable you to successfully apply coaching within your team and create the coach-enabled leaders of the future.

Being coach-minded and time to act

Two major themes have evolved from the line manager and team leader interviews relating to the experience of the MAC or coach-like leader, as distinct from the supportive points contained in the conceptual framework of Figure 6.1. These are: *be coach-minded* and *time to act*; their characteristics are outlined in Table 9.1 and Figure 9.1.

The coach-minded approach is representative of how the line managers and team leaders responded in their interviews to team challenge, with clear guidelines relating to their learned analyses: *the way a manager or leader needs to be if they wish to employ a coach-like style.* Pulakos et al. (2015) reiterate that the manner in which a manager or leader conducts themselves in everyday scenarios should be reflective of the required behavioural standards in the team – *walk the talk* and set an observable example. The line manager and team leader interviews noted that their own emotional stability aided their ability to combat challenge, as endorsed by other observers (e.g. Hur et al. 2011) when facing similar conditions relating emotional intelligence (*being tenacious and having self-belief*) with empathy (*having emotional intelligence*), motivation and self-awareness (*starting with self*). This supports other research that emotionally stable people tend to use successful conflict-resolution strategies to resolve any disagreements by involvement of fellow team members (Radley and Chamberlain 2001), and by being open and remaining transparent about their desired outcome. One interviewee defined the purpose and role of a *coach-minded manager* as:

> Instinctive psychologists understanding personality and motivation as the main building blocks of the individual psyche, they understand what they are dealing with in terms of personal profile and traits and how to use the human factor.

This confirms that a combination of a personal-focused approach and utilizing the skills and individual qualities of team members will likely create a fully functioning team. This defines the relevance and importance of *the human factor*.

Time to act is representative of how the interviewees viewed the urgency with which team challenge needs to be addressed to prevent escalation and a negative impact on the team. The speed of action protects the credibility and reputation of the line manager or team leader when confronting a challenging scenario, and is perceived as being supportive of the team members in the

Table 9.1 Characteristics of being coach-minded

Data analysis—being coach-minded		Time to act	Potential impact	Conduct
be a leader role model	prevent chaos / manage conflict	address issues at source	prevent chaos/ manage conflict	be impartial / be professional
address issues at source				
have professional expertise– be credible	be confidential when required	know when to step in	prevent chaos/ manage conflict	be confident when required have self-belief
be open and honest–admit when you are wrong	empower as much as possible			
be credible		don't allow situations to escalate	risk loss of credibility	mitigate pain for team members / draw upon inner resource
be impartial				
don't pretend you have not seen something–deal with it	don't allow situations to escalate	don't pretend you have not seen something–deal with it	risk loss of credibility / be seen to be open and honest	be principled / don't be manipulative
know when to step in	be humble			
empathize	be principled			
don't be manipulative	start with self	deal with challenge– don't put it off	lead from within	start with self / have self-belief
tackle performance issues immediately	draw upon your inner resource			
mitigate pain for them	have EI	tackle performance issues immediately	gain tenacity and credibility	get them to the point where they answer the issue / be humble have / EI/empathy
be tenacious and have self-belief	be self-aware / own awareness			
deal with challenge–don't put it off	get them to the point where they answer the issue			

Figure 9.1 Being coach-minded and time to act

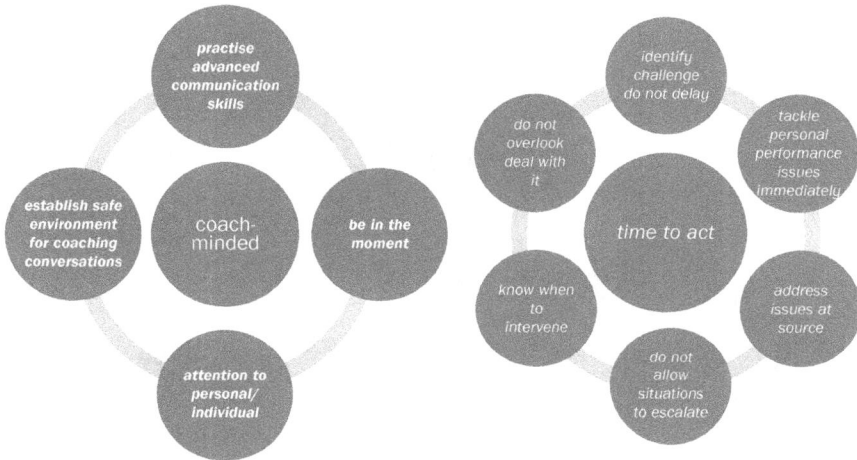

expectation that the right course of action has been pursued for the benefit of the team. Not acting in addressing a team challenge was not viewed positively and could lead to victimization of individual team members. There is also a strong potential for diminishing performance due to a feeling of disenfranchisement, with team members not wishing to cover for a colleague not dealt with by the line manager or team leader.

One of the pivotal requirements of a coach is to place the interests of the coachee first, and a speedy response may be viewed as supportive of the wellbeing of that individual and their team members. The efficient functioning of a team is sustained by not overlooking issues and addressing them at source. If the issue is deemed to be of a personal nature, it's important not to ignore the opportunity to intervene or to allow the situation to escalate. The issue needs to be dealt with immediately. The intent to *intervene, when to intervene* and *how to intervene* is regarded as an essential step to divert a team member from potentially unproductive or dysfunctional behaviour. The interviewees placed the responsibility for maintaining this approach with the line manager or team leader, with statements such as *being a manager means you are responsible, take decisions, govern, sometimes you have to just take control.* Accordingly, the following framework encompasses the contributory factors reported by the line managers and team leaders interviewed, for being coach-minded *and* the need for immediacy in maintaining a functioning and responsive team. The Team Challenge Framework is illustrated in Figure 9.2 and can be viewed as offering the responsible line manager or team leader a practical coaching-based guide for dealing with team challenge.

The support framework encompasses the collective response from the interviewees within the conceptual framework (Figure 8.1) of the team effectiveness models (Table 3.1) and the contributory factors leading to unproductive or dysfunctional behaviours (Table 5.1). If negative behaviours are left unaddressed,

Figure 9.2 Team Challenge Framework

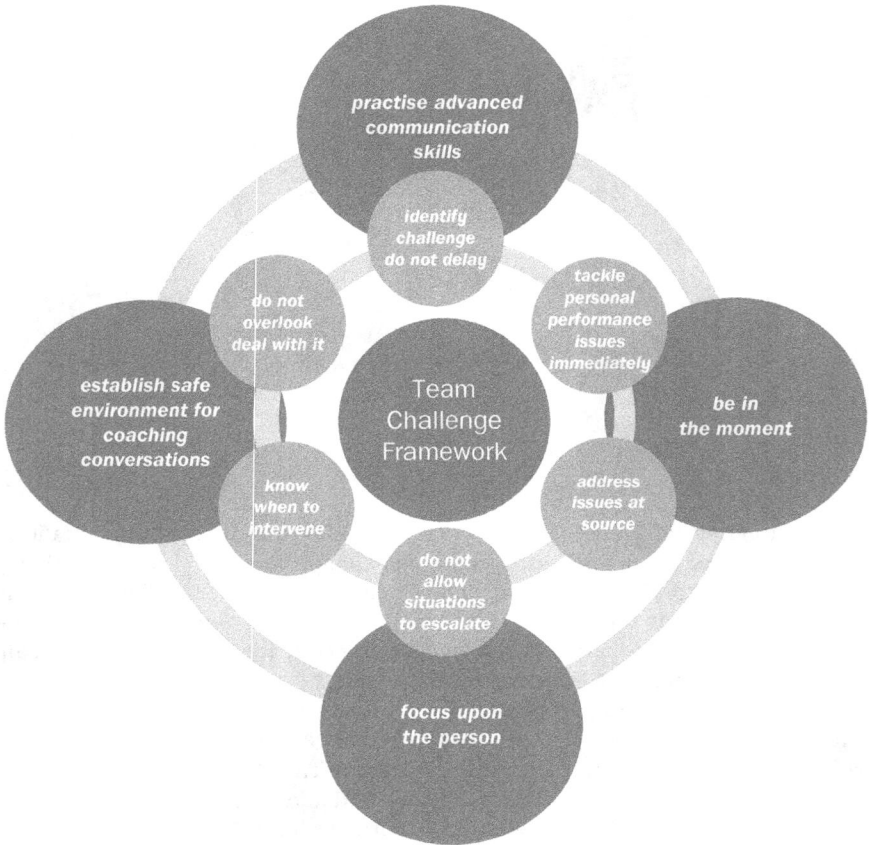

the impact on the efficient functioning of the team can impair organizational purpose and the credibility of the line manager or team leader in terms of an abrogation of responsibility and failure to support the team. One interviewed manager endorsed the following:

> *Backstabbing and bitching behind backs without even having a conversation is a no-go in my team. We just do not do it. I just don't tolerate that at all. So, if those sorts of things come to me, I stamp them out really early.*

From analysis of the line manager and team leader feedback, the evolution to coach-minded conduct and its prescriptive responsibilities is illustrated in Figure 9.3 emphasizing the need to display a positive leader role when addressing behavioural issues.

The consequences and contributory factors relating to this analysis will be examined further. When analysing contemporary literature, it is clear why the

Figure 9.3 Evolution of attributes linked to coach-minded conduct

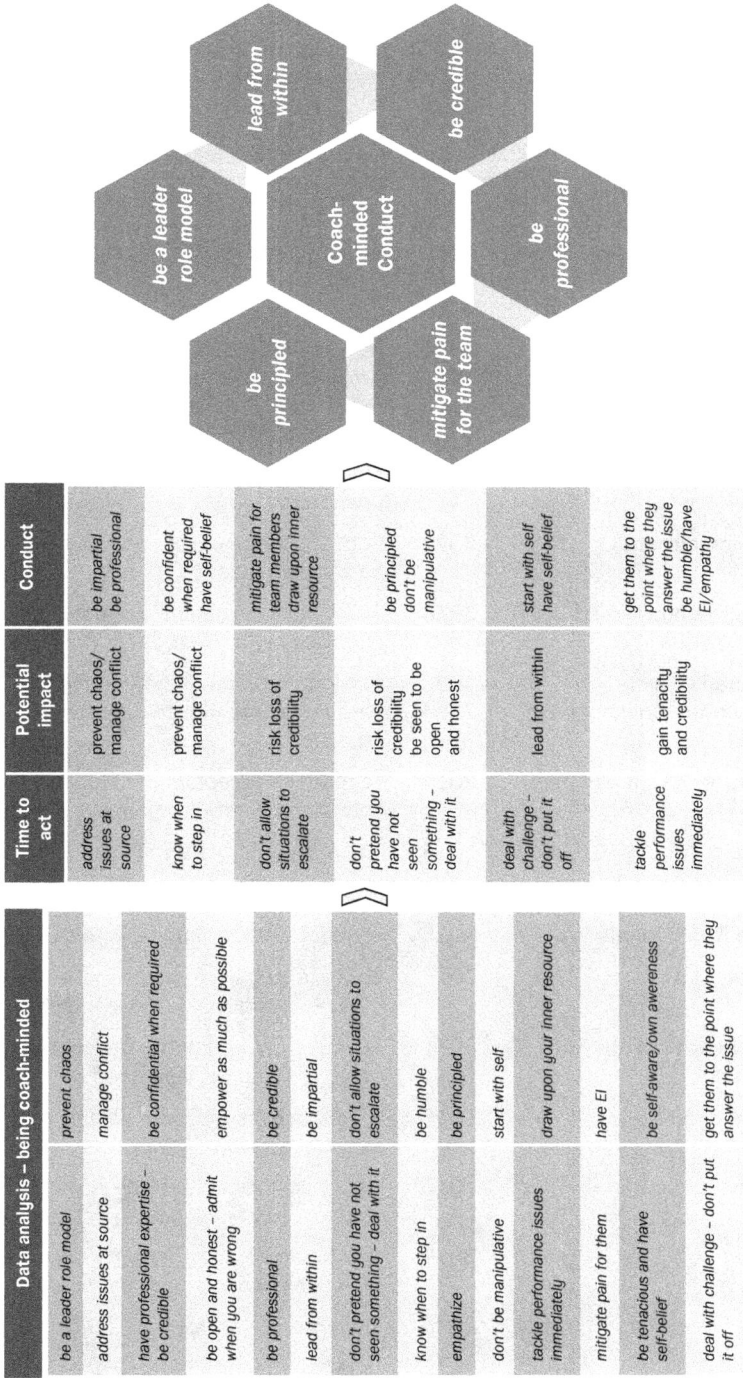

Data analysis – being coach-minded	Time to act	Potential impact	Conduct
be a leader role model prevent chaos			
address issues at source manage conflict	address issues at source	prevent chaos/ manage conflict	be impartial be professional
have professional expertise – be credible be confidential when required			
be open and honest – admit when you are wrong empower as much as possible	know when to step in	prevent chaos/ manage conflict	be confident when required have self-belief
be professional be credible			
lead from within be impartial	don't allow situations to escalate	risk loss of credibility	mitigate pain for team members draw upon inner resource
don't pretend you have not seen something – deal with it don't allow situations to escalate	don't pretend you have not seen something – deal with it	risk loss of credibility be seen to be open and honest	be principled don't be manipulative
know when to step in be humble			
empathize be principled			
start with self	deal with challenge – don't put it off	lead from within	start with self have self-belief
tackle performance issues immediately draw upon your inner resource			
mitigate pain for them			
be tenacious and have self-belief be self-aware/own awereness	tackle performance issues immediately	gain tenacity and credibility	get them to the point where they answer the issue be humble/have EI/empathy
deal with challenge – don't put it off get them to the point where they answer the issue			

expectation and investment in a MAC or coach-like leader for training the requisite coaching skills is high. Table 9.2 presents the required competence and anticipated abilities of a MAC or coach-like leader, as summarized from the literature.

Table 9.2 Anticipated abilities of a MAC or coach-like leader

Authors	Yr.	Anticipated Abilities of MAC
Batson & Yoder Ewen et al. Fairhurst & Connaughton	2012 2013 2014	To *form good relationships*
Anderson Kim	2013 2014	Role model–esp. tasks and skills, requires *occupational self-efficiency* (OSE) Role model–*most important ability* *Behave to influence desired change*
Auer et al.	2014	*Manage and mitigate different sources of uncertainty*
Engelbrecht et al.	2014	*Self-regulate, motivate self and others and be socially adept*
Karacivi and Demirel	2014	*Be empathetic and have emotional intelligence*
de Haan et al. Fairhurst & Connaughton	2013 2014	Provide *regular informal feedback* Be able to *give constructive developmental feedback*
Fairhurst & Connaughton	2014	To manage *receptors of meaning* when communicating with team members
Petrie	2014	To possess a *global mindset*
Al-Nasser & Mohamed	2015	*Enable people to work together*
Dello Russo et al.	2016	To *reduce organizational politics in teams*
Gerard et al.	2017	Be a vital cog in organizational sustainability through dialogue-focused leadership
Engelbrecht et al.	2014	Ability to self-regulate, motivate self and others and be socially adept
Salas et al.	2015	To *encompass thoughts, feelings and behaviour towards joint goals*
Savelsbergh et al.	2015	*Be supportive and provide non-defensive responses to questions and challenges*
Sun et al.	2017	Be able to communicate for *each team member to understand team purpose*
Yang	2015	*Influence social sharing*
Zoltan	2015	Deliver a *higher order of leadership*

From this analysis, the conduct and personality of the line manager or team leader are key enablers to achieve the anticipated *desired* outcomes, as endorsed by the interview data. In this exploration, half the interviewees were not formally trained in coaching but nevertheless employed an instinctive coach-minded style, as one interviewee states:

> The manager today has a much more important task. They need to do every-thing, including walking on water; because they need to be psychologists, they need to be technically sound, they need to have all the soft skills.

An appropriate line manager and team leader role model should be embed-ded within the culture of the organization as an antecedent and benchmark for employees. The characteristics listed in Table 9.2 offer a template for the organization and for managers and leaders to create the necessary mindset to achieve the organizational goals. The creation of a positive mental closeness or shared mindset becomes part of the supportive role of a line manager or team leader in evolving a functional team (Zoltan 2015).

Role modelling of line manager and team leader in dealing with team challenge

The role of a line manager or team leader in developing a coach-minded approach when dealing with team challenge merits attention. As defined by the interviewees, the adoption of the Team Challenge Framework (Figure 9.2) provides an evolution of the prescriptive elements in Figure 9.1 and supports a requirement to define a suitable model for the role of line manager and team leader. Being self-aware as a leader and manager was identified as an import-ant requirement for the role, offering an opportunity for team members to observe and develop new insights into attitudes and behaviours at work by comparing the consequences of their own actions and behaviour with their col-leagues (Yang 2015). This role modelling does not exclude the team leader or line manager; as one interviewee stated, *leaders have followers*, thus the need to be self-aware, be humble, be careful to communicate through *role model-ling* to others in the team on knowing how to interact, as this is a vital part of *leading from within*. The interview data reveals characteristics such as being *impartial, open* and *humble* as a team leader and being *credible* and *profes-sional*. As one manager reported:

> You're open to change as a manager and that change being informed from your team not from a typical management team but actually from people who are doing this role on a day-to-day basis.

This would suggest a true synergy with what is going on in the team, being aware enough to notice changes or being able to divert errors or actions that are not aligned. This awareness was seen as contributory to the line manager or team leader being professional and credible, thereby setting the standard of expected behaviour.

Leadership characteristics of a MAC or coach-like leader

The chameleon nature of the MAC and coach-like leader became clear when discussing team challenge, as in some instances the interviewees reported that the manager was required to step into a leadership role, and queried:

> *Who are you when you are coaching – are you still a manager?*

The choice of manager versus leader when applied in the context of MAC is important when dealing with team challenge. Coaching has evolved from the management perspective of a task-focused process to a robust leadership concept (coach-like leadership) with an additional psychosocial behavioural focus (Zoltan 2015). One interviewee expressed this as:

> *The Manager focuses on the what and how, but the Leader focuses on the why.*

Clarity on when to adopt a coach, managerial or leadership role is fundamental to fulfilling the expectations of the MAC and coach-like leader as reflected in the anticipated abilities summarized earlier in Table 9.2. One interviewee explained the role as:

> *I have a three-pronged approach. In today's business, you cannot function without three hats. And that is the hat as a leader which is being inspirational, influencing and giving people a sense of direction; being a manager which is controlling, understanding what's going on and putting systems in place so that we can actually manage what's going on, manage budgets and manage projects, but also a coach is the third one which is actually about empowering people, engaging people to take them out of their comfort zones and perform at a greater level. So, it's those three hats ... of manager, leader and coach. I don't believe you can run today's businesses effectively and really fully maximize the potential of the business and the people unless you've got those three hats on.*

Table 9.3 identifies the respective role descriptors of manager and team leader model in addressing team challenge as supported by the pragmatic response from the above interviewee.

The coaching approach supports the leadership stance with a required focus on people and influence to address behavioural challenge through reasoning

Table 9.3 Role of manager vs. leader

Role of the manager How and when?	Role of the leader What and why?
tasks, actions, operational management	people, influence, business objectives
short-term/operational efficiencies	long-term/strategic positioning
doing things right –> first time	doing right things –> in future
plan actions, organize and implement	plan direction, inspire and motivate
follow processes/systems	implement entities/structures

and cognitive restructuring. Adopting the role of the line manager provides focus on tasks and actions rather than behaviour, while that of a team leader is more about inspiring and motivating, which are attributes more likely to counter unproductive or dysfunctional behaviour. While the interview data supports coaching as a leadership skill, the dilemma for some managers is that being coach-minded requires the behavioural attributes of the *leader role model* which may induce a stressful or overwhelming expectation for this higher level of competence. In this instance the line manager has to resist reverting to a *tell and command* position and be sure to utilize the dialogue and stance of a coaching approach, ensuring engagement and empowerment of the team member. Several interviewees adopted a conscious leadership stance to deal with team challenge, which necessitated the action of *taking control*, but in a qualified manner.

The potential conflict in the role-model expectation of a MAC or coach-like leader is illustrated in Figure 9.4 and reflects an inability to address challenge due to the difficulty of switching *seamlessly* between the roles of coach, leader and manager. In this circumstance, the dilemma is that the individual may not necessarily possess the experience to recognize the appropriateness or application of each role, to feel comfortable flowing between one and the other.

Figure 9.4 Potential conflict of role models

One interviewee noted:

The manager as coach has another role and that is leader.

This leader role applies when the MAC or coach-like leader steps up to deal with an evolving situation within a team in a coaching manner, thus averting any scenario that may inhibit the operational efficiency of the team. Dealing with challenge, identifying the primary provoker of conflict and addressing unproductive or dysfunctional behaviour will require the line manager or team leader to be tenacious and draw on their inner resources to manage and lead such situations with surety and authority. The interviewees per se were practised, knowledgeable, comfortable in leading and positive instigators of the coaching process, which enabled them to deal with many of the challenges as presented. In support, the term coach-like leadership (Karaçivi and Demirel 2014) appears more appropriate when addressing challenge. The distinction between MAC and coach-like leadership is a valuable new insight which requires clarification, wider communication and acceptance as to its relative importance and significance in the ability to deal with challenge, engender support and create a positive outcome. One perspective could view the MAC as a generic term capturing the elements of coaching from the standpoint of an orderly, task-focused, prescriptive relationship-building process. As there will be occasions when a manager needs to *take control*, the coaching elements will follow to ensure that the required process of dialogue and action is replicated to engender continuity. Alternatively at times, the dialogue of coaching and managing may appear in conflict for a line manager or team leader as the development of the individual may be at odds with attainment of an immediate task in operational management, as expressed by the following statements:

> I think you can be a leader-coach and you can be a manager and you can be a manager-leader, but I'm not sure you can be a manager-coach. I think being a manager means that largely you are responsible, you take decisions, you govern if you like. But if you adopt the role of leader, then you support others to do that.
> One of the difficulties that organizations are having at the moment is in trying to generate the manager-coach, is that maybe no such person can exist. And that you need to separate out these skills so that if you're going to be a coach to your people, then you have to adopt the role of leader rather than manager.

These statements describe the quandary that some managers feel when they are expected to coach. The dilemma is ever likely to continue if this descriptive conflict is not addressed. Accordingly, the modern concept of coach-like leadership relies on the MAC being emotionally intelligent and line managers being empathetic in fulfilling the requirements of relationship building. Another commentator in this field, Dello Russo et al. (2016), listed *coaching leaders* as mitigating organizational politics to enable fully functioning teams. One interviewee elaborates:

If you intend to coach your team members you need to adopt the role of coach-leader; if you are going to take responsibility for their actions vs. allowing them to take their own, then you adopt the role of manager.

In combination, these comments suggest a level of competence and leadership ability to best leverage the benefits of coaching when dealing with challenge. Consequently, the coach-like leader will have characteristics such as reflection *to be able to do the right thing*, asking how to create the optimum environment or space for the team to work collectively (Al-Nasser and Mohamed 2015), how to promote the team to socially share (Yang 2015), build relationships (Batson and Yoder 2012; Ewen et al. 2013; Fairhurst and Connaughton 2014), facilitate knowledge exchange and learn from each other. The managers and leaders interviewed supported Engelbrecht et al. (2014) who recognized that managers who self-regulate are better able to motivate their team members, which is an identified leadership trait. Therefore, coaching as a leadership rather than a management role seems more fitting. Another authority in this field, Ciporen (2015), describes coaching as a partnership process *not usual in hierarchical, control and command relationships* which guides an individual team member through personal development, creating alignment between the needs and intentions of the individual and the organization such as *people and business objectives – as in the role of the leader, what and why*. This coaching leadership role is expressed in the following comments from the interviewees:

Get people to behave in ways that support the organizational needs.
Invest and look for ways to improve individual productivity by understanding what holds them back and create a bespoke solution.
The thing I have learned is that people don't take ownership if they are managed; if you lead then you are placing responsibility upon them to take ownership. Lead vs. Manage!

Taking ownership in a dynamic, fast-paced team environment is essential and, according to the data, can only be achieved through leadership. Another interviewee was adamant that the level of emotional intelligence required to lead in such a manner is a *layer above just being self-aware – it's about processing in an even, balanced way*. Consequently, from this feedback s*tarting-with-self* is vital to be credible, and to possess the required individual focus to *know team members well enough* to *mitigate pain* and *create bespoke solutions*. Additional quotations that place the MAC dealing with team challenge within the definition of leadership are:

When leaders do not listen, they lose themselves as great leaders. Leadership is as much about listening as it is about giving the narrative. It's about being able to find ways to empower people to be part of the solution, so they have emotional buy-in which then gives you flexibility. Ultimately, it's about finding people you can empower to take the organization forward. Let them make

mistakes, work closely with them, and help them recover from mistakes, support them, draw out talent.
Teams need leaders not managers. Management is a function, a task function. Leadership is much broader and much more focused on outcomes vs. task. I think the qualities of a leader are much more required for the person who is involved with the development of the team ... a team can manage itself, it does not actually need a manager. Whereas a leader in a team can help to bring out the best in the team members, a manager in a team is much more likely to impose their way of doing things on the team. And that is going to limit the potential of the (individual and) team.

Another author on coaching, Suriyankietkaew (2013), states that coaching represents a shift in managerial philosophy, challenging the one person-centric model in favour of greater reciprocity, as supported below:

Act as a leader from an informed place.
Look after people first from a place of respect.

This shift in philosophical stance can create internal challenge and lack of focus for some managers and team leaders. To mitigate this, Table 9.4 provides a listing of the specific actions and associated rationale required of the line manager or team leader in dealing with team challenge according to interview data based on the MAC or coach-like leadership actions.

These required actions and rationale can be condensed into a quick reference document for line managers and team leaders to self-assess their competency in dealing with team challenge. Details and actions can be associated with each of the MAC or coach-like leader actions (knowing, appreciating, assessing, intervening) as represented in the quick check template illustrated in Figure 9.5.

An important attribute of being coach-minded and being a coach-like leader begins with an appreciation of the individual's contribution to team success, which requires the line manager or team leader to know their team. The insight gained from this research is built from an understanding that individual team members in the organization require the line manager or team leader to possess a global inclusive mindset (Petrie 2014) to capture all potential factors that impact the well-being and functioning of their team members.

From a practitioner perspective, being coach-minded and knowing the time to act (Figure 9.1) and the evolved Team Challenge Framework (Figure 9.2) are themes which provide an insight into the operational success of the team effectiveness models in addressing unproductive or dysfunctional behaviour.

The self-assessment checklist in Table 9.5 can further be used by the practitioner as a precursor for addressing team challenge by assessing the level of competence and questioning the response to the MAC actions as previously outlined. This mirrors the approach a coach-minded line manager or coach-like team leader would adopt in meeting the above challenge.

Table 9.4 Actions and rationale for dealing with team challenge

MAC actions	Action to deal with team challenge	Rationale
Knowing (foster confidence) ✓ know your team ✓ know your team well ✓ really know your staff ✓ know their ambitions and drivers	• start with *knowing self – reflect* • *have professional expertise* *Then...* • *know your team* • *know your team well* • *really know your staff* • *know their ambitions and drivers* • *acknowledge people* • *hold many perspectives*	• to lead *from within and be credible & maintain self-awareness* • to understand all facets of team & facilitate full alignment • *to connect meaning with individual ambitions* • *to be empathetic* • *to be professional* • *to have confidence in decision-making & gain consensus* • *be confident to challenge* • *to show commitment to the team* • *to empower individuals and the team*
Appreciating (foster humility) ✓ staff are different ✓ characteristics ✓ people & issues ✓ culture & grievances ✓ what is important to staff	• *staff are different* • *characteristics* • *people & issues* • *culture* • *grievances* • *what is important to staff* • *staff potential* • *if change is required*	• to facilitate appreciative relationships between team members of their differences – to leverage cooperative behaviour • to encourage empathy and build team spirit • to provide clarity of role & responsibility required of each team member to enable increased effort and commitment • *make staff feel valued* • *to be straight and honest*

(Continued)

Table 9.4 (Continued)

MAC actions	Action to deal with team challenge	Rationale
Assessing (foster learning)	• details/facts • what's going on • importance • mistakes & learn • is change required	• to be able to create a safe environment for coaching conversations • to communicate honestly and effectively on their level • to create harmony • to define roles clearly • to enable self-sustainable team
✓ clarify details/facts ✓ unpick the details ✓ soak up what's going on ✓ importance		
Intervening (foster exchange)	• know when to act • be in the moment • manage conflict • deal with challenges – don't put off • don't allow situations to escalate • be transparent • enable and develop staff (partner) • balance friendly & supportive	• to be a leader role model • to have coaching conversations: discuss, reason, robust dialogue • to provide information on when and how • to foster collaboration • to create open supportive environment • to get them to the point where they know the answer • to build trusted relationships – interpersonal focus • to foster enthusiasm and passion – self and team
✓ when to act		

Figure 9.5 Understanding your team

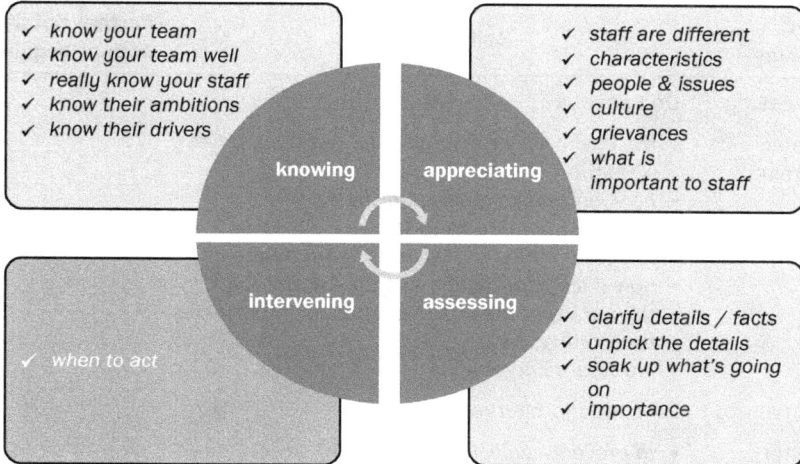

- ✓ know your team
- ✓ know your team well
- ✓ really know your staff
- ✓ know their ambitions
- ✓ know their drivers

knowing **appreciating**

- ✓ staff are different
- ✓ characteristics
- ✓ people & issues
- ✓ culture
- ✓ grievances
- ✓ what is important to staff

intervening **assessing**

- ✓ when to act

- ✓ clarify details / facts
- ✓ unpick the details
- ✓ soak up what's going on
- ✓ importance

Table 9.5 Self-assessment for dealing with team challenge

MAC actions	Self-assessment	Further details/ actions required
Knowing	Do I know?	
(foster confidence)	• whether my behaviour exhibits the desired role model • whether I demonstrate commitment to my team • whether I am viewed as empathetic • how to communicate with each team member (language, tone) • what motivates my team members • individual characteristics and personalities • how to inspire teamwork and collaboration • how to empower individuals • what, how and when to challenge • whether my approach is viewed as professional	
Appreciating	Do I appreciate?	
(foster humility)	• that staff are different • different characteristics and personalities • diversity • how team members interact • staff potential and individual ambitions • the importance of making staff feel valued • and acknowledge individuals • when to be transparent	

(Continued)

Table 9.5 (Continued)

MAC actions	Self-assessment	Further details/ actions required
Assessing (foster learning)	Do I assess? • the environment suitability for learning, privacy, dialogue • how individuals react to mistakes • how the team reacts to failure / success • the contribution of individual team members • how each contribution supports team goals • the nature of the challenge and its importance • role compatibility • intrateam interactions	
Intervening (foster exchange)	Do I need to intervene? • to prevent conflict • to foster collaboration • to prevent escalation of inappropriate situations • to deal with challenge • to enable and develop individual staff • to provide information of when and how • to address unproductive or dysfunctional behaviour	

Practitioner application

The following interview statement endorses the benefits of knowing your team members through being coach-minded and focusing on the individual, their characteristics, their abilities, their needs and the required attributes while supporting them in achieving the organizational objectives. The added dimension of being person-focused, with its associated insight, facilitates leverage in challenging situations for the line manager or team leader, as illustrated in the following statements:

> I would probably, when dealing with a challenge, tend to have individual conversations before team conversations. Because of the different personalities I don't know whether I would do that if my team was more aligned in personality traits ... So, what I tend to do, if I know I have different personalities in the team and something needs to be discussed within the team that is going to be difficult, I would have individual discussions first to take the initial hit from the fiery ones and brief and compare with the less confident ones. By the time you get everyone together, everyone has had a chance to breathe a bit and then have a discussion that's meaningful and productive. If I don't know their personalities, I can't do that.

You have to develop your people. You have to spend time developing them, and if I look back on the company, one of the big things that they are driven by is growth, and growth of the company comes from growth of the people.

Knowing your team is a pivotal requirement to address differences, promote team sharing, collate knowledge, assess different ways of doing things and gain information. The research data confirmed the need to know your staff to facilitate conversations, reasoning, persuading, influencing and enabling them as individuals to gain potential for broadening their mindset towards *cognitive restructuring*. In the absence of an enabling structure, unproductive and dysfunctional behaviour could go unnoticed and spiral out of control, affecting the operational success of the team.

This exploration has established that the primary challenge in modern teams is rooted in personal differences and potential for conflict, and supports the need for a capable and confident *leader role model* to have constructive coaching conversations to address differences at the earliest opportunity. Knowing your team members would be the precursor to make this possible by having an interest in the individual. Creating a positive mental closeness or collaborative mindsets between team members becomes part of the manager's essential role in evolving a functional team (Zoltan 2015).

The advice from the expert line managers and team leaders who employ a coaching style supports the need for an early coaching-style intervention and conversation. As a coach, knowing your team members well acts as a precursor to addressing differences. One statement from the data relates to being coach-minded as *allowing people to step into their power*, which requires the line manager or team leader to be aware of their capability and trust the individual. This awareness is only possible by having an interest in and understanding of the individual. If the line manager or team leader adopts this coaching approach, they will be fully informed of the team status and will know when to act. Knowing their team members, they will be able to appreciate the situation, assess its seriousness or severity and intervene accordingly; see Figure 9.6.

These requirements can be classified as advanced communication skills. In coaching, *hear patterns* in what is being said, *ask the right questions* to get to

Figure 9.6 Knowing when to act

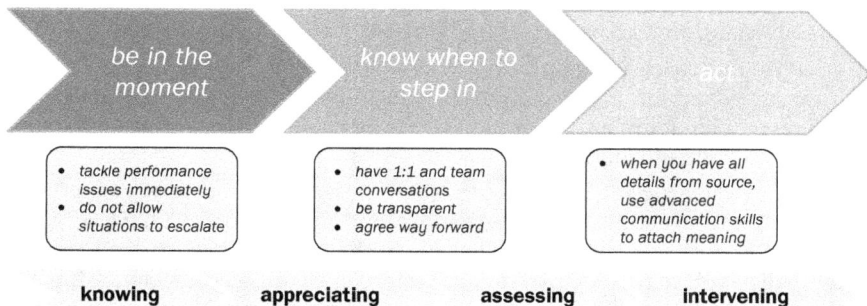

be in the moment	know when to step in	act
• tackle performance issues immediately • do not allow situations to escalate	• have 1:1 and team conversations • be transparent • agree way forward	• when you have all details from source, use advanced communication skills to attach meaning

knowing   **appreciating**   **assessing**   **intervening**

the facts, *get a feel for things* for subsequent evaluation, *highlight the level of attention* required by the line manager or team leader to engage, *be present* and *possess the awareness and humility* to ask the right questions, *be appreciative* and *assess the important issues* prior to intervention. Coaching as actioned by the line manager or team leader provides a means to model a role by providing a template for building the appropriate skill set within the team. This will assist in moving towards the *point of them knowing what the answer is* and solving the problem for themselves. Knowing when to act provides a trigger point that line managers and team leaders need to recognize to prevent the potential of negative outcomes such as unproductive and dysfunctional behaviour. This will further protect and maintain the correct functioning of the team in a timely manner (Hall 2013).

Irrespective of title, being coach-minded is required to achieve success in the desire to support and enable others, to be collaborative, to be humble and to address unproductive and dysfunctional behaviour. Being coach-minded is a choice for the line manager or team leader, but it is hoped that the details shared from the 30 interviews from managers and leaders who employ a coaching style offer you a starting point to achieve your own fully functioning team.

Use the self-assessment as a starting point and try this approach when resolving team issues. You may be overwhelmed at your own and your team's success.

Reflective questions

- What 'chameleon'-like behaviours have I developed, and how do I know? Which behaviours are the easiest for me? Which are the hardest for me? What circumstances do I find myself in when it is hard for me to flex my chameleon-like behaviour set? What might I do to develop these further?

- What am I learning about any conflicts that are generated between my standard management behaviours and when I attempt to use my coaching behaviours? What have I tried so far to manage these? What else can I try to reconcile these conflicts?

- What role models am I creating in my teams, which demonstrate the chameleon character of effective manager and coaching behaviours? How effective are they, and what else can I do to create visible role models?

- What do I do to capture my learning or insights about patterns in the teams? To what extent am I creating my own safe spaces to review and reflect on my own behaviours and approaches? What evidence am I proactively generating to help me judge this?

- What have I learned about the types of questions to ask, and how/where/when to ask these questions? What situations and people need to have a higher level of attention than others? What might that tell me about those scenarios and the people involved? How might I intervene in those scenarios to tap into the potential of those involved to release wider team performance?

Summary

This book is based on the practical experience of 30 line managers and team leaders from multiple disciplines who use a coaching approach to gain the best from their teams. The in-depth interviews deal with the challenge of modern-day teams (diversity, dynamics, building trust, alignment, time, ownership and responsibility) which hopefully is relevant and resonates with your experiences as regards what creates challenge for you and your team.

The journey has taken us through the reported primary challenges faced in the current business environment and lays the foundation for the unique approach that managers use to assist in being individually focused in uniting their team. These team challenges lead to consideration of the external pressures that impact organizations and teams: resource scarcity, employee demands and team configuration. The latter point of team configuration has afforded the opportunity to look at the established knowledge about teams and performance through the lens of understanding team effectiveness, appreciation of what enabling structures are, consideration of the elements of a safe team environment, clarity of direction to enable interpersonal focus, and from a team leader and manager perspective how to foster collaboration and trust through a universal understanding of the desired outcomes.

Comparing and contrasting the insights from the interviewees enabled another view of what it means to be a leader versus a manager, with reports of a dual role and a conscious choice of when each is adopted versus the alternative. The primary drivers of the leadership or management decision lead to team cohesion, increased engagement of the team members, and fostering collaboration and sharing. How these decision-point scenarios are dealt with impacts the team members' perception of organizational support and illustrates the importance of the team leader, the influence of the manager and their behaviour, as referenced in the section on the behavioural and management practice of the team leader. The section further highlights the manager and leadership understanding of dysfunctional behaviour, leading to an appreciation of which type of organizational culture creates this behavioural anomaly.

Professional organizations such as the Chartered Institute of Personnel and Development place managers and team leaders front and centre of people management and development on behalf of their employers, which creates an internal environmental demand from their employers and team members. Line manager expectations have led to the evolution of the manager as coach (MAC) with identification of the required characteristics and development of individuals to be more understanding, to be adept at creating alignment and developing healthy functional relationships between themselves and team members. The demand for a change in mindset for managers, leaders and team members requires a foolproof process and systems that can assist in achieving a trusting and functional team, pointing to coaching as a potential solution.

In conclusion, the interview data has provided a blueprint for dealing with team challenge through fostering trust, accountability, commitment from team members and creating a safe environment for open conversation in appreciation of individual contributions to the team. Once this foundation of mutual understanding and appreciation is in place, it's a straightforward step to establish clarity of direction both for the team and individually. This enables the coaching interpersonal focus as a tailored support for each team member. Problem-solving and enhanced learning then becomes part of the routine since clarity of direction aligns and drives everyone towards collaborative team working and desired outcomes. This adds to the improved learning capability across the team through open conversation, trust and problem-solving dialogue.

The insight from the data has generated templates and guidance in support of the appreciation and importance of knowing our team, how to be coach-minded and how to conduct ourselves as leaders and managers as we aspire to employ coaching as our modus operandi.

Kindly review and utilize the templates, models, checklist and self-assessments to enable us to glean further insight regarding their application from a practitioner's perspective. Make these tools your own, modify them to your needs and assess their success.

Please share your insights with the wider community, since collaboration is a must in our fast-paced environment. We hope this small contribution to your leadership and management quest helps you develop a fully functioning team.

We welcome feedback on your progress and wish you well in your endeavours.

References

Al-Nasser, A. and Mohamed, B. (2015). Examining the relationship between organizational coaching and workplace counterproductive behaviours in the United Arab Emirates, *International Journal of Organizational Analysis*, 23(3): 378–403. DOI: 10.1108/IJOA-08-2014-0793.

Anderson, V. (2013). A Trojan horse? The implications of managerial coaching for leadership theory, *Human Resource Development International*, 1(16): 251–66. DOI:10.1080/13678868.2013.771868.

Auer, J.C., Kao, C.-Y., Hemphill, L., Johnston, E.W. and Teasley, S.D. (2014). The uncertainty challenge of contingent collaboration, *Human Resource Management Journal*, 24(4): 531–47.

Batson, V.D. and Yoder, L.H. (2012). Managerial coaching: a concept analysis, *Journal of Advanced Nursing*, 68(7.6): 1658–69. doi: 10.1111/j.1365-2648.2011.05840.x.

Ciporen, R. (2015). The emerging field of executive and organizational coaching: an overview, *New Directions for Adult and Continuing Education*, 2015(148): 5–15.

de Haan, E., Duckworth, A., Birch, D. and Jones, C. (2013). Executive coaching outcome research: the contribution of common factors such as relationship, personality match, and self-efficacy, *Consulting Psychology Journal: Practice and Research*, 65(1): 40–57. DOI:10.1037/a0031635.

Dello Russo, S., Miraglia, M. and Borgogni, A. (2016). Reducing organizational politics in performance appraisals: the role of coaching leaders for age-diverse employees: OPPA and coaching leadership, *Human Resource Management*, 56(5): 769–83.

Engelbrecht, A.S., Heine, G. and Mahembe, B. (2014). The influence of ethical leadership on trust and work engagement: an exploratory study, *SA Journal of Industrial Psychology*, 40(1): article 2010. https://doi.org/10.4102/sajip.v40i1.1210.

Ewen, C., Wihler, A., Blickle, G. et al. (2013). Further specification of the leader political skill – leadership effectiveness relationships: transformational and transactional leader behavior as mediators, *Leadership Quarterly*, 24(4): 516–33.

Fairhurst, G. and Connaughton, S.L. (2014). Leadership: a communication perspective, *Leadership*, 10(1): 7–35. DOI: 10.1177/1742715013509396.

Gerard, L., McMillan, J. and D'Annunzio-Green, N. (2017). Conceptualising sustainable leadership, *Industrial and Commercial Training*, 49(3): 116–26.

Hall, J.L. (2013). Managing teams with diverse compositions: implications for managers from research on the faultline model, *Advanced Management Journal*, 78(1): 4–10.

Hur, Y., van den Berg, P.T. and Wilderon, C.P.M. (2011). Transformational leadership as a mediator between emotional intelligence and team outcomes, *Leadership Quarterly*, 22(4): 591–603.

Karaçivi, A. and Demirel, A. (2014). A futuristic commentary: coach-like leadership, *International Journal of Business and Social Science*, 5(9): 126–33.

Kim, S. (2014). Assessing the influence of managerial coaching on employee outcomes, *Human Resource Development Quarterly*, 25(1): 59–85.

Petrie, N. (2014). *Future Trends in Leadership Development* [white paper]. Greensboro, NC: Center for Creative Leadership. Available at: https://lean-construction-gcs.storage.googleapis.com/wp-content/uploads/2022/09/08152942/Future_Trends_in_Leadership_Development.pdf (accessed 23 January 2023).

Pulakos, E.D., Hanson, L.M., Arad, S. and Moye, N. (2015). Performance management can be fixed: an on-the-job experiential learning approach for complex behaviour change, *Industrial and Organizational Psychology: Perspectives on Science and Practice*, 8(1): 51–76.

Radley, A. and Chamberlain, K. (2001). Healthy psychology and the study of the case: from method to analytic concern, *Social Science and Medicine*, 53(3): 321–32.

Salas, E., Shuffler, M.L., Thayer, A.L., Bedwell, W.L. and Lazzara, E.H. (2015). Understanding and improving teamwork in organizations: a scientifically based practical guide, *Human Resource Management*, 54(4): 599–622. DOI: 10.1002/hrm.21628.

Savelsbergh, C.M.J.H., van der Heijden, B.I.J.M. and Poell, R.F. (2010). Attitudes towards factors influencing team performance, *Team Performance Management: An International Journal*, 16(7/8): 451–74. http://dx.doi.org/10.1108/13527591011090682.

Sun, H., Pei-Lee, T. and Karis, H. (2017). Team diversity, learning, and innovation: a mediation model, *Journal of Computer Information Systems*, 57(1): 22–30.

Suriyankietkaew, K. (2013). Emergent leadership paradigms for corporate sustainability: a proposed model, *Journal of Applied Business Research*, 29(1): 173–82.

Yang, I. (2015). The positive outcomes of 'Socially Sharing Negative Emotions' in work teams: a conceptual exploration, *European Management Journal*, 34(2): 172–81.

Zoltan, R. (2015). Group dynamics and team functioning in an organisational context, *Ecoforum*, 4(2): 154–8.

Appendix

ID	age band	profile
1	60+	Professional coach, manager researcher and author
2	40+	High street bank talent development – ex-Army, not formally trained as a coach, extensive team management training and experience
3	50+	Ex-pro vice chancellor – challenging environment – consultancy – not coach trained
4	50+	Worked across multiple sectors as leader – most challenging voluntary sector – trained coach with professional accreditation
5	50+	Professionally trained coach (ICF) – some consultancy, HR lead on turnaround project in dysfunctional SME
6	60+	Professional coach (ICF) with vast managerial experience – challenge leading a volunteer team
7	50+	Ex-trainer and manager for retail sector – consultant coach and trainer
8	60+	Consultant, ex-journalist, coach trained to Master Practitioner level – member of EMCC
9	60+	Consultant, engineer, trainer and higher education tutor – no formal coach training, vast management training and experience
10	50+	Project manager of offshore teams – difficult environment, safety driven – newly trained coach
11	50+	Regional healthcare manager, uses coaching and mentoring interchangeably to assist teams – no formal coach training
12	30+	Newly appointed project manager – dealing with dotted line management challenges – not coach trained, but management trained
13	50+	Professional executive coach – consults within teams and management to support team development
14	40+	HR consultant, presently acquiring coach qualifications – previous leadership based on training background
15	40+	Educational manager – not formally coach trained, but very coach aware and management trained

ID	age band	profile
16	60+	Professional coach – process- and project-driven manufacturing background – consultant for major manufacturing organizations
17	40+	Talent development lead at a major healthcare trust – previous county council employee, coach trained
18	60+	Professional manager, coach trained
19	30+	Human resource online tutor, team leader
20	40+	University manager – not coach trained, mindfulness and EI trained
21	50+	Manager of an IT team – accountability to others and others' deadlines, coach trained
22	50+	Human resource lead at a university – coach trained
23	60+	Coach trained librarian – lead librarian for UK university libraries
24	70+	Ex-teacher turned mentor – no formal coach/mentor training
25	60+	Professional manager – NLP trained, coach aware, challenge of leading a remote team
26	40+	Human resource manager at a North West university – coach trained
27	40+	Supervisor, educator – no formal coach training, team management experience
28	40+	Army commanding officer – moved from team to team troubleshooting
29	40+	Newly appointed CEO of a dysfunctional team – turnaround process in hospice
30	50+	Consultant, manager – coach trained member of ICF professional coaching body

Index

Page numbers in italics are figures; with 't' are tables.